Cambridge Elements ≡

Elements in Historical Theory and Practice
edited by
Daniel Woolf
Queen's University, Ontario

THE THEORY AND PHILOSOPHY OF HISTORY

Global Variations

João Ohara
Federal University of Rio de Janeiro

CAMBRIDGE
UNIVERSITY PRESS

Shaftesbury Road, Cambridge CB2 8EA, United Kingdom

One Liberty Plaza, 20th Floor, New York, NY 10006, USA

477 Williamstown Road, Port Melbourne, VIC 3207, Australia

314–321, 3rd Floor, Plot 3, Splendor Forum, Jasola District Centre,
New Delhi – 110025, India

103 Penang Road, #05–06/07, Visioncrest Commercial, Singapore 238467

Cambridge University Press is part of Cambridge University Press & Assessment,
a department of the University of Cambridge.

We share the University's mission to contribute to society through the pursuit of
education, learning and research at the highest international levels of excellence.

www.cambridge.org
Information on this title: www.cambridge.org/9781009005159

DOI: 10.1017/9781009036313

First published 2022

A catalogue record for this publication is available from the British Library.

ISBN 978-1-009-00515-9 Paperback
ISSN 2634-8616 (online)
ISSN 2634-8608 (print)

The Theory and Philosophy of History

Global Variations

Elements in Historical Theory and Practice

DOI: 10.1017/9781009036313
First published online: August 2022

João Ohara
Federal University of Rio de Janeiro

Author for correspondence: João Ohara, Ohara.jrm@gmail.com

Abstract: This Element argues for a broad and inclusive understanding of the "theory and philosophy of history," a goal that has proven elusive. Different intellectual traditions have competing, often incompatible definitions of what could or should count as proper "theory/philosophy of history." By expanding on the traditional versions of the "history of the theory and philosophy of history" and including contexts from the Global South, particularly Latin America, the author hopes to offer a broader, more inclusive perspective on the theoretical reflections about history.

Keywords: theory of history, philosophy of history, philosophy of historiography, historical theory, historical thinking

ISBNs: 9781009005159 (PB), 9781009036313 (OC)
ISSNs: 2634-8616 (online), 2634-8608 (print)

Contents

1 Introduction

Philosophy of history, theory of history, and historical theory are three existing labels that are sometimes, but not always, treated as synonyms.[1] Each of these has been used by both historians and philosophers to define a specific field of inquiry, which entailed its own approaches, methods, concepts, and problems, as well as specific venues and audiences, though these often overlap each other. As such, it is difficult to state clearly which label has been used by which community for what ends. Furthermore, a quick look into the massive bibliography compiled by the *International Network for Theory of History* will demonstrate the wide variety of themes and authors that, in different intellectual traditions, have come to be considered part of the theory or philosophy of history. But despite a somewhat shared intuition that these activities are linked by some sort of family resemblance, recent attempts at formulating a general definition to a unified field have yet to show any evidence of success in articulating these diverse agendas.

I believe that discussing such articulations can help us foster a rich and diverse intellectual community dedicated to questions of the utmost importance for our ways of dealing with a thoroughly historicized world. Therefore, this Element is dedicated to just this task: arguing for a broad and inclusive understanding of the theory and philosophy of history. I will begin with an exploration of the various ways that different intellectual traditions have understood the phrases "philosophy of history," "theory of history," and "historical theory," and then consider whether and how we could achieve a broad and inclusive understanding of those terms, an understanding I believe can be covered by the phrase "theory and philosophy of history." Of course, there is a limit as to how detailed my exposition can be in this format, but I will make sure to point readers to the relevant contemporary literature where they can find further interesting material.

Section 2 is dedicated to surveying the most familiar understandings of "philosophy of history," "theory of history," and "historical theory" for Anglophone readers. First, I will deal with the pretty conservative story that starts with what became known as "substantive" or "speculative" or "material" philosophies of history (up to the early twentieth century), goes through the "analytical" or "critical" or "formal" phase (from early to mid-twentieth century), and culminates in "narrativist" philosophy of history (in late-twentieth century).

---

[1] Not to mention some cases where the idea of "theoretical reflection" about history is joined with the history of historiography. In this Element, however, I will cover only partially this approximation, when we get to the senses in which some historians understand the label of "theory of history."

I will then point to how this traditional story depends on a specific definition of "philosophy of history," one which has persisted even after it was allegedly superseded by a new one, that of the narrativists. The persistence of this definition explains why this story ignores or pays only cursory attention to then-contemporary developments in France and Germany, to earlier neo-Kantian philosophy of culture and other late historicists, or to the whole lineage of epistemological and methodological reflection by historians themselves. I will then deal with what historians mean by "historical theory" or "theory of history." As we will see in due time, these labels have come to mean either the study of the many different facets of history or the discussion of concepts and ideas borrowed from neighboring disciplines, such as social theory, literary theory, and so forth. Discussions of "theory of history" have also inherited some of the contents of "methodology" and "historiography" manuals, which often began with nineteenth-century "positivist" or "traditional" historiography (i.e., Ranke in Germany, Langlois and Seignobos in France), went through the successive generations of the *Annales*, the British Marxist historians, and ended with twentieth-century New Cultural History. In this sense, the relationship between historians and theoretical reflection is one characterized by some instrumental, operative interest, and a great deal of suspicion of "epistemology."

In Section 3, I will explore how Latin American intellectuals have dealt with theoretical and philosophical reflections on history. There, the traditional categories of "philosophy of history," "theory of history," and "historical theory" reach their limits, not because of any kind of intrinsic inadequacy, but precisely because of important local developments in former colonial spaces whereby subjects tried to understand their (post)colonial condition and their place in the modern world. The "universal history" of modern Europeans often had no place (or only a marginal one) for these (post)colonial subjects, and this situation endowed (post)colonial thought with an inherent historical dimension to it, an awareness of their (and of others') historicity. Though I will point to the fundamentally historical aspect of postcolonial critiques of modernity, my focus will be on the works that Latin American intellectuals have explicitly related to labels like "philosophy of history," "theory of history," or "historical theory." Even such a limited exploration will already be relevant for my claim that any effort toward a wide and inclusive field of "theory and philosophy of history" should take into account the challenges that have been presented by traditions outside North America and Western Europe and in languages other than English.

Finally, in Section 4, I will consider whether and how a broad understanding of the "theory and philosophy of history" could be achieved. After exploring the different kinds of questions that have been posed under the umbrella terms of "philosophy of history," "theory of history," and "historical theory," a clear and rigorous definition of the field becomes either impossible or institutionally undesirable: There is no one set of necessary and sufficient conditions that ultimately characterizes "theory and philosophy of history," and the limited definitions that are possible fail to account for large portions of the work that is currently being done under the relevant labels. These limited definitions also make it unlikely that such narrow enterprises have any chance of institutional survival and growth. Nevertheless, I will argue that we can put forward a broad understanding of "theory and philosophy of history" that covers a wide range of areas of inquiry loosely connected in virtue of being interested in our varied modes of relations to the past(s), with the price being that of abandoning the search for common agendas and vocabularies and instead embracing the idea of a common space of exchange.

2 The Traditional (Hi)stories of the Theory and Philosophy of History

By the first half of the twentieth century, the label "philosophy of history" had come to designate works dedicated to discovering the purpose, meaning, direction, or the general laws of history as a whole (understood here as the course of past events). Though the phrase had been coined by Voltaire in the eighteenth century, works from other authors were soon fit into that category: from Augustine to Bossuet and Vico, from Condorcet to Oswald Spengler and Arnold Toynbee. Of course, the methods by which one could find the ultimate purpose, meaning, direction, or laws of history were varied, and they sometimes involved at least some empirical material. But in the context of postwar Anglophone philosophy, dominated as it was by analytic philosophy and, perhaps most importantly, logical empiricism, such philosophical task was rather seen with suspicion – to say the least. It is telling that R. G. Collingwood's *The Idea of History*, a posthumous edition of his lectures published in 1946, began with a distinction between Collingwood's use of the term and those of previous philosophers. As W. H. Walsh later stated, "a writer on philosophy of history, in Great Britain at least, must begin by justifying the very existence of his subject" (Walsh 1960: 9). But that seemed to be the case even across the Atlantic: In his 1938 book *The Problem of Historical Knowledge*, Maurice Mandelbaum too had thought it necessary to state clearly what was the nature of his philosophical inquiry. The fundamental distinction then was between the philosophy of the whole course of past events and the philosophy of our knowledge of those events – or, as these postwar philosophers formulated it, between speculative and critical, substantive and analytical, or material and formal philosophies of history.

This distinction was usually expressed by an analogy with that between the philosophy of nature and the philosophy of science. As Walsh stated, "the first is concerned to study the actual course of natural events, with a view to the construction of a cosmology or account of nature as a whole. The second has as its business reflection on the whole process of scientific thinking, examination of the basic concepts used by scientists, and matters of that sort" (Walsh 1960: 14). Much as nature was the legitimate object of science, so was history the legitimate object of historiography. Were philosophers to study nature or history, they would be doing either science/historiography (instead of philosophy) or metaphysics. On the other hand, were they to study the concepts and reasoning of scientific/historiographical inquiry, then they would be closer to logic and epistemology.

But most importantly, this distinction was not merely about differentiating areas of philosophical interest. Rather, it differentiated between what those philosophers considered to be *legitimate* philosophical interests (logic, epistemology) and illegitimate ones (metaphysics) (see Ahlskog 2018: 87–88). As Jonathan Gorman noted, philosophers trained in the analytic tradition considered that "the whole speculative approach had been successfully squashed by the Vienna Circle in the 1930s and, with particular respect to the philosophy of history, squashed later by Karl Popper and Isaiah Berlin" (Gorman 2018: 62). Therefore, it should come as no surprise if, by the 1950s and 1960s, important books in analytical philosophy of history contained at most passing, quick references if any to the "speculative" branch – see, for instance, Dray (1957, 1966), or White (1965), or collective volumes such as Hook (1963) and Gardiner (1974).[2] To be sure, Arnold Toynbee's *A Study of History* sparked lively debates over whether or not one could empirically determine the general pattern of past events (see Mandelbaum 1948 and Geyl, Toynbee, and Sorokin 1949). Meanwhile, Karl Jaspers' *The Origin and Goal of History* was translated and published in 1953 – only four years after its original publication in Germany. But by the time Karl Popper published *The Poverty of Historicism*, in 1957, "speculative" philosophy of history was indeed a disappearing genre in the Anglophone world – at least as far as (analytical) philosophers were concerned.[3]

---

[2] Kerwin Lee Klein offered an alternative reading: For him, it was the broad editorial success of *speculative* philosophy of history that made it possible for *analytical* philosophy of history to exist after World War 2. (Klein 2011: 42–47).

[3] The ambition of finding large, all-encompassing patterns in history remained present in other forms. Francis Fukuyama and the whole discussion around the "End of History" in the 1990s are usually mentioned as examples (see Paul 2015a, Ahlskog 2018). We could extend things even further by considering the allure of Deep or Big History, such as with Yuval Noah Harari's 2011 bestseller *Sapiens*, and the wide resonance of David Graeber and David Wengrow's 2021 book

2.1 From Analytical to Narrativist Philosophy of History

In contrast to the perceived decline of the "speculative" philosophy of history, the "critical" or "analytical" branch flourished due to the debate around historical explanations – that is, whether historical explanations have the same logical structure as scientific explanations. It is rather usual to claim that Carl Hempel's 1942 paper, *The Function of General Laws in History*, marks the beginning of the critical philosophy of history (see, for instance, Kuukkanen 2021: 2, Ahlskog 2018: 88, Gorman 2018: 67, and many of the chapters in Brzechczyn 2018, just to mention some of the most recent accounts). In his paper, Hempel claimed that contrary to the belief that history "is concerned with the description of particular events of the past rather than with the search for general laws which might govern those events ... general laws have quite analogous functions in history and in the natural sciences" (Hempel 1942: 35). According to this model, scientific explanations took the form of a deductive argument where the initial conditions and the relevant general laws acted as premises from which one could deduce the conclusion (or final state) – hence its name, deductive-nomological or "covering-law" model. For Hempel, then, "in history as anywhere else in empirical science, the explanation of a phenomenon consists in subsuming it under general empirical laws" (Hempel 1942: 45).

In the following two or three decades, the questions of whether history followed (even partially) the general model of scientific explanation conceived by Hempel and the logical empiricists and whether there were aspects specific to historical explanations fueled a debate in which historians were mostly absent and one which they mostly ignored (see Klein 2011: 52–53). Whether historians thought the model was a good representation of their practices was irrelevant. The main issue at stake was one about the logical structure of historical explanations: Was there something about them that deviated from general scientific explanations? Despite some philosophers having expressed thoughts about the importance of studying explanations that historians actually offered, the debate remained highly abstract and mostly confined to philosophers themselves (e.g., Gardiner 1952, Dray 1957, Goldstein 1976). In turn, historians either ignored the debate altogether or complained that the deductive-nomological model did not fit the way practicing historians explained things – both reactions had little importance for philosophers.[4] However, by the late 1960s

---

The Dawn of Everything. But then again, the name, philosophy of history, is still gone – not the least because these more contemporary grand-pattern-finding enterprises claim to be empirically based (is any resemblance to Spengler and Toynbee mere coincidence?).

[4] See the great account by Jonathan Gorman (2018: 69–70 and 2021: 27–28) of J. H. Hexter's review of Danto's book *Analytical Philosophy of History* and Morton White's *Foundations of Historical Knowledge* and the authors' reaction to it.

and early 1970s, these discussions had lost steam. For Gorman, by then, "those few analytical philosophers who had taken a special interest in historical understanding seemed to have drawn all they could from their brief excursion into thinking about historiography" (Gorman 2021: 26).

To be sure, the philosophy of history was not the only (and certainly not the most important) front where logical empiricism and the covering-law model faced challenges. For instance, Thomas Kuhn's 1962 *The Structure of Scientific Revolutions* seemed to challenge some of the core assumptions of the kind of philosophy of science championed by Popper, Hempel, and the logical empiricists, and many historical and sociological approaches to the sciences claimed to be heavily influenced by it.[5] But most importantly, the whole problem of historical explanation faded out of interest for analytic philosophers: The explanation/understanding debate "had found a new home in a freshly established branch of philosophy," the philosophy of action, where historiography ceased to be the source of relevant cases (D'Oro 2008: 412), and the project of the unity of science as envisioned by the logical empiricists was mostly abandoned, rendering obsolete the discussion over whether historical explanations followed the covering-law model or not. Meanwhile, an interest in the narrative structure of historical writing gradually occupied the space that the analytic philosophers had left vacant.

The story of when and how the main debate in the philosophy of history turned from historical explanation to the narrative structure of historical writing, or we could also say from analytical to narrativist philosophy of history, usually reserves a prominent place for Hayden White's 1973 book *Metahistory* – and not without reasons (White 1973). Though other authors have contributed to this general shift, such as Louis Mink (1987) and Frank Ankersmit (1983), *Metahistory* had a profound impact beyond the narrow limits of the philosophy of history as analytic philosophers understood it. White's positions elicited responses from historians and literary critics from many different countries and intellectual traditions in a way that none of the analytical philosophers of history had until then.[6] By 1986, Ankersmit was able to write, boldly, that

> if philosophy of history is content to become an odd positivist fossil in the contemporary intellectual world within the next few years, by all means let it remain epistemologist. If, on the other hand, philosophers of history have the

---

[5] Though it is common to include Kuhn's *Structure* among the possible factors in the decline of logical empiricism, the issue is, as usual, more nuanced. For some of the different interpretations, see Larvor (2000), Rorty (2000), and Salmon (2000) as well as Bird (2015) and Richardson (2015).

[6] For the reception of Hayden White, see Vann (1998), Avelar (2018), and Domańska and La Greca (2019). Franzini (2017) covers the reception of White in Brazil, and Carrard (2018) in France.

courage to shake off their own past and entertain a sincere wish to contribute to a better understanding not only of historiography but also of the problems that are currently under debate in other philosophical disciplines, it cannot avoid becoming narrativist (Ankersmit 1986: 27).

The interest in "narratives" was not exactly new when *Metahistory* was published. For a while then some of those involved in the analytical philosophy of history were exploring the idea that historical explanations frequently assumed the form of a narrative, or that at least some components of historical explanations had to be understood by their narrative qualities. Arthur Danto's famous article "Narrative Sentences" had been published in 1962. W. B. Gallie's own intervention appeared a year later, arguing that historical understanding was "the exercise of the capacity to follow a story" (Danto 1962; Gallie 1963: 193).[7] However, *Metahistory* changed the main object of the philosophy of history. Rather than considering these narrative elements in a general epistemology of history, White pushed for "a linguistically inspired theory about historical writing" (Paul 2011: 81).[8] This, along with Ankersmit's (1983) book *Narrative Logic* and Mink's important essays later collected in the 1987 volume *Historical Understanding*, paved the way for a new agenda for the philosophy of history – that of *narrativism*[9] (see also Klein 2011).

Though "narrativism" itself can be a quite contested label, commentators have usually referred to Hayden White and Frank Ankersmit as the proponents of its two main variants.[10] Finding common denominators among those classified as narrativists is a challenging ordeal,[11] but a fair starting point might be their focus on the fundamental and constitutive role of language in historical writing (and later thinking). In the case of White, this involved a particular theory of our historical imagination, that is, of the processes by which we transform raw materials of our present experience into data about the past and

---

[7] Vann (1995) offers a detailed account of this transition to narrativism, one which benefits from his long experience as editor of *History and Theory*.

[8] On the same page, Herman Paul states that this new approach was a "turning point in postwar philosophy of history" and that it "would definitely change the agenda of (especially English-language) philosophy of history."

[9] It is worth mentioning that, for Richard Vann, Mink's 1966 essay, rather than White's *Metahistory*, seems to mark the beginning of narrativism, or at least of the linguistic turn in the philosophy of history. Paul (2011) and other studies of White's work are usually clear about the close intellectual relationship between White and Mink. It is also worth mentioning Hans Kellner and Frank Ankersmit's 1995 edited volume *The New Philosophy of History*.

[10] Sometimes, others have been included in this classification, such as Louis Mink, Paul Ricœur, and even David Carr – these last two sometimes being further characterized as "phenomenological narrativists." Importantly, Herman Paul (2011: 109) and Kalle Pihlainen (2017: xvi et seq.) have raised concerns over the merits and problems of the label.

[11] See, for instance, Paul Roth's (2016) assessment of Jouni-Matti Kuukkanen's (2015) definition of the narrativist position.

then organize (or "emplot") the relevant parts into a followable story – a theory that has important consequences, as we shall see next. Meanwhile, for Ankersmit, narrativism involved understanding the representational aspect of historiography, that is, its ability to represent (at least aspects of) the past through a narrative text – a task that compelled him to turn to the philosophy of language and an aesthetical account of historiography.[12]

In *Metahistory*, White proposed to "consider the historical work as what it most manifestly is – that is to say, a verbal structure in the form of a narrative prose discourse that purports to be a model, or icon, of past structures and processes in the interest of *explaining what they were by representing* them" (White 1973: 2, emphasis in the original; see also White 1986: 81–83). His general analysis dealt with the poetic procedures by which historians prefigured the "historical field," that is, turned the chaos of experience into an ordered space populated by discrete and defined objects, and then transformed this "data" into a followable story, one "emplotted" in one of four general tropes (White 1973: 30 et seq.; see also White 1999: 8–9). But most importantly, White insisted that this emplotment was a moral or aesthetic, rather than epistemological matter. Plots were features of stories, not events, and, at least in principle, historians could choose between different modes of emplotment depending on what kind of story they were telling (see White 1973: 6, note 5, and 427; see also White 1987: 43–44 et seq.).

For Ankersmit, however, literary theory cannot account for what he sees as the most fundamental problem, that of the relation between language and reality. In his view, this problem should rather be dealt with through an engagement with the "linguistic turn" as brought forth by philosophers such as Richard Rorty and W. V. O. Quine, that is, with the rejection of the empiricist distinction between analytic and synthetic truths, and with the idea that "in history truth may have its origins in the compulsions of language no less than in those of experience" (Ankersmit 2001: 37). As such, Ankersmit dedicated many of his writings to the problem of historical representation, whereby aesthetics rather than epistemology seemed to provide the best tools for those philosophers of history interested in understanding how historians could possibly represent aspects of the past in their writings (see, for instance, Ankersmit 1994, 2001, and 2012).

The problems of historical representation, the metahistorical prefigurative structures of historical imagination, and the epistemological, ethical, and aesthetical implications of these theses stimulated a rich and diverse body of

---

[12] For more detailed analyses of White's work, see Tozzi (2009), Paul (2011), La Greca (2013). For Ankersmit, see Bos (2018), Paul and van Veldhuizen (2018), Menezes (2019, 2021). For a good introduction to narrativism, see Tozzi (2022).

responses. For some historians, White and other narrativists had downplayed much of what distinguished the writing of history from the writing of fiction and, as such, misrepresented the cognitive labor involved in searching for, organizing, and making sense of a wide range of documents. They thought that narrativism entailed blurring the line between real historiography and fiction, which was either unacceptable, misleading, or just plain wrong (e.g., Kramer 1989, Chartier 1997, Lorenz 1998, Evans 1999, Breisach 2003). Perhaps the most famous challenges came from those who worried about what narrativism might entail to the history of the horrors of the twentieth century, particularly those of the Holocaust (see Friedländer 1992, Kansteiner 1993).[13] White, Ankersmit, and other narrativists responded to some of these criticisms, but whether their responses were successful or not is still a contested issue. Nevertheless, the narrativist insight inspired a great number of articles, monographs, and edited volumes exploring both its theoretical workings and how they fared against the history of historiography.[14]

Many philosophers remained skeptical that narrativism had any *philosophical* relevance. For them, it remained unclear what the connection was between the narrative structures of historical texts and the logic of historical explanations or the epistemology of historical understanding (see, for instance, Roth 2016 or even Ankersmit himself on the literary theory-inspired variation of narrativism, Ankersmit 2001: 64 et seq.). Others thought it important to deal more directly with the skeptical conclusions or interpretations of the narrativist theses (e.g., Carr 1991, McCullagh 1998 and 2004, Tucker 2004). It is important to remember that many of the analytic philosophers that were engaged in the debate of historical explanations had simply abandoned the field. Anecdotally, Danto mentioned that, as editor of the *Journal of Philosophy*, he estimated that only "one per thousand submissions" to the journal were related to the philosophy of history (Danto 1995: 72).[15] Despite Ankersmit's continued engagement with certain groups within analytic philosophy, it did not take long before philosophers were not the dominant group on the pages of *History and Theory* anymore.

---

[13] Though Kansteiner later found White's narrativism useful to understand Saul Friedländer's widely acclaimed *The Years of Extermination*. See Kansteiner (2009).

[14] It would be impossible to give an exhaustive list, but some suggestions are Bann (1984), Kellner (1989), Rigney (1990), Ankersmit (1994), Kellner and Ankersmit (1995), Harlan (1997), Megill (2007), Ankersmit, Domańska and Kellner (2009).

[15] Aviezer Tucker objected to the idea of there being a crisis in the philosophy of history during the 1980s and 1990s (Tucker 2001). Also, the main group of researchers behind the INTH has found that the absolute number of publications indicate "an overall growth of publications over the last seventy years" (Bevernage et al. 2019: 413). However, because by now we lack a clear definition of "philosophy of history," "theory of history," and "historical theory," any such assessment is bound to be of limited use. Bevernage et al. explicitly declare that they join all these together.

And this is where our traditional story ends. Not because narrativism represents the culmination of our philosophical progress, but rather because at least from the 1990s onward, debates in the philosophy of history simply lack a clear central focus. Some authors have tried to give an overview of this rather diverse situation. For example, Chris Lorenz has argued that these new themes and problems are related to the decade's memory boom (Lorenz 2012: 26 et seq.). As such, questions about the metaphysics, ethics, and politics of our relations to the past have reentered the agenda amidst calls for decolonization, reparations, intergenerational justice, environmental catastrophe, and so on. Though Lorenz's assessment seems fair, I have doubts as to whether this new moment can still be easily labeled under the "philosophy of history" label – at least as analytical philosophers of history and narrativists understood it.

Other authors have preferred to differentiate between those works by philosophers, which deal with traditional philosophical questions, and those by "theorists of history," whose inquiries are not "self-evidently philosophy of history." Contrary to other optimistic views on the current state and future of the former group, in Jouni-Matti Kuukkanen's view, it is the latter that is experiencing a boom in recent years. For him, "theory of history" includes themes like "trauma, memory, experience, new forms of history-writing, use of history, etc., which have not been traditional topics in explicit philosophical studies. And it is fair to say that these investigations are not either the kinds of explicit conceptual explorations that many associate with philosophy" (Kuukkanen 2018: 73–74; see Klein 2011: 53–58 for an alternative view). Though I tend to agree with Kuukkanen's assessment and with his general perception of a difference to be had between these different kinds of work, I will also argue later that this distinction is semantic rather than substantive. For now, let us turn to what I believe to be some of the limitations of the traditional story we tell about the philosophy of history.

2.2 Demarcating the Philosophy of History

As we have seen, the traditional story of the philosophy of history usually starts with Anglophone philosophers distinguishing their work from what was then condemned as "substantive" or "speculative" philosophy of history. It often refers to authors like Maurice Mandelbaum or R. G. Collingwood but fails to mention that both were engaged in a debate that stemmed from late nineteenth-century neo-Kantianism, one that was still alive by the early twentieth century. Mandelbaum's *The Problem of Historical Knowledge* was entirely about what the author saw as the historical relativism of Croce, Dilthey, and Mannheim, and the insufficient responses to such relativism given by Simmel, Rickert, Scheler, and Troeltsch. Likewise, in *The Idea of History,* Collingwood engaged with ones like Windelband, Rickert, Dilthey, Bergson, Croce, and others. However, despite all this, debates in the analytical philosophy of history mostly ignored further developments in continental thought about history and the "cultural sciences" – Gallie (1963, 1964) being one notable exception. Though Ernst Cassirer's *Das Erkenntnisproblem in der Philosophie und Wissenschaft der neueren Zeit* was translated and published by Yale University Press in 1950, analytical philosophers of history, in general, showed no interest in what they probably considered to be part of the "failed programme" of idealism. Even Collingwood had to be "adjusted" to the new empiricist framework of analytic philosophy (Skodo 2013: 158–59 and Klein 2011: 50).

The very label "analytical philosophy of history" is confusing. "Analytical," "critical," and "formal" were ways of distinguishing a kind of philosophy of history from its "speculative," "substantive," or "material" variants, and they had approximately the same meaning, that is, the philosophical (conceptual, logical) analysis of the "science of history." But the label "analytical philosophy of history" has also been used with other meanings in different contexts. It has been used to point to analytic philosophy as an intellectual tradition or an approach to (or a style of doing) philosophy since many of those involved in it were analytic philosophers,[16] but it also appeared as naming a period, rather than an agenda or a style of doing philosophy (of history). In this sense, it meant the period that started in the 1940s and ended in the 1960s and 1970s, depending on whether we consider the beginning of narrativism to be Mink's "The Autonomy of Historical Understanding" or White's *Metahistory.* This time frame does coincide with what we could emplot as the "growth and decline" of the analytic approach to the philosophy of history, but the distinction between a period and an approach to philosophy matters. For instance, we find almost no discussions of Raymond Aron's *Introduction à la Philosophie de l'Histoire*, published in France in 1948 and translated to English only in 1961, or Henri-Irénée Marrou's *De la Connaissance Historique*, published in 1954 – both examples of a "critical" variety of the philosophy of history, though not devoted to the problem of historical explanation nor strictly related to the tradition of analytic philosophy. As such, these and other books remain excluded from the discipline history of the philosophy of

---

[16] As Kerwin L. Klein wrote, "those grounded in the British idealist tradition, from Walsh to Louis O. Mink, called their practice 'critical' philosophy of history. Those trained in the post-Wittgensteinian linguistic tradition, from Carl Hempel to Morton White, spoke of the 'analytical' philosophy of history" (Klein 2011: 42). For a while now, "analytical" has been the most common choice between the two.

history in English. Either in its German or French variety, debates with the "continental" tradition have only reappeared later, with the arrival of narrativism.

Historians are also absent from the traditional story of the philosophy of history – at least until the narrativist turn (see Marnie Hughes-Warrington's intervention in Clark et al. 2018). Nothing about the *Historik* genre, which was an important part of German nineteenth-century historiography, J. G. Droysen's being its most known adept (Blanke et al. 1984). Even the British, famously resistant to "theorization," had their share of ink spilled over what historical knowledge was (see, for instance, Elton 1967, Carr 1987). However, these were not always considered to be relevant by analytical philosophers of history. For example, Aviezer Tucker claimed that "understanding historiography or science requires understanding what historians or scientists are doing, not what they think they are doing," and later cited Leon Goldstein's statement that "historiography is what historians write as historians, not what they say they do" (Tucker 2004: 4, Goldstein 1996: 256). From positions such as these, it is not surprising that almost no historian was mentioned as an interlocutor during the reign of the analytical philosophy of history. Indeed, being committed to the study of "what historians actually do" does not entail considering "what they say they do" as evidence of that. From the point of view of analytic philosophers of history, if the reflexive texts historians wrote fell short of being philosophical or philosophically interesting, then indeed they had no reason to be part of the history of the philosophy of history.

All these exclusions start to make sense when we consider that the traditional story of the philosophy of history merely extended the narrow account of the analytical philosophy of history. Given how its participants defined the field, these exclusions were justified in the history of analytical philosophy of history. But they became problematic when the demarcation criteria were changed by the rise of narrativism. The meaning of "philosophy of history" for the narrativists is not the same as for the analytic philosophers. Narrativists championed a "new philosophy of history" indeed but then the distinctions and exclusions held by their analytic predecessors were no longer justified. Though narrativists were certainly more open to continental philosophy and had a different position toward "what historians say they do," their disciplinary story remained unchanged. In other words, though their understanding of what counted as "philosophy of history" changed, this had little effect on their retrospective accounts of a disciplinary history of the philosophy of history. To use Hayden White's terms, they did not choose another past more in line with their present criteria of demarcation.

2.3 Current Proposals for the Philosophy of History

The philosophy of history remains at the margins of mainstream analytic philosophy, and we have no reason to believe this will change in the near future.[17] Though the label still exists, it has been used interchangeably with "theory of history" more often than not. However, some philosophers have raised doubts over whether much of the work that claims to be part of the "philosophy of history" really is *philosophy*. As I have mentioned earlier, Kuukkanen is among those who raised the question most clearly. He perceives a difference between "philosophy of history" and "theory of history," meaning by the latter the study that focuses more "on social phenomena and changes in it, such as new modes of presenting history, and on coming to terms with the consequences of these changes." In this sense, "it is not often very precise conceptually and not aware enough of ('analytic') philosophical uses of concepts and terminology" (Kuukkanen 2018: 79–80). Kuukkanen's distinction is fairly reasonable in that he recognizes that what he calls "theory of history" is a very different undertaking from the "philosophy of history" if we take the analytic "style" of philosophy as the standard definition for "philosophy."[18] Participants in the debate now come from many different departments and intellectual traditions, and they pose a wide range of questions that does not and cannot fit into how analytic philosophers define "philosophy." I will discuss later the issue of conflation between "philosophy of history" and "theory of history," but I believe it is important to look at how philosophers of history have defined their field in more recent times.

Back in 2004, Aviezer Tucker published *Our Knowledge of the Past: A Philosophy of Historiography*, where, for the sake of clarity, he chose to use the phrase "philosophy of historiography" whenever the object of philosophical study is our knowledge of past events. He offered right from the start some clear definitions that are meant to disambiguate the problems that come with our ordinary language use of the word "history." Most important for our present discussion is this: "By history I mean past events. *Historiography* is composed of representations of past events … *Scientific historiography*, the main topic of this book, is historiography that generates probable knowledge of the past" (Tucker 2004: 1, emphases in the original). His distinction is clear and well stated, and it follows approximately the same structure that "critical" or

---

[17] About the lack of interest by mainstream analytic philosophy in the philosophy of history, see D'Oro (2008). For a reasonable assessment of the future possibilities for the philosophy of history in philosophy, see Tucker (2010): 80–82 – though, as most of the time, this seems to apply mainly to philosophers in the United States and the Anglophone world more broadly.

[18] Of course, Kuukkanen himself notes that "analytic philosophy" is a rather fuzzy term in its own right.

"analytic" philosophers of history had used in the past. As such, the "philosophy of historiography" is understood as a subfield of epistemology just like the philosophy of science.[19] Tucker's proposed solution for the ambiguity of the word "history" has attracted other philosophers, such as Kuukkanen (2015, 2018) precisely because it offers a seemingly simple way of defining the actual object of philosophical analysis. Of course, he claims to not share the "obsolete philosophical positions and distinctions" that characterized the previous "analytical" or "critical" versus "substantive" or "speculative" distinction, but still holds to what I consider a questionable separation between epistemology and metaphysics (Tucker 2009: 3).[20] Despite any reservations, Tucker's definition of the "philosophy of historiography" has the advantage of following something like a standard understanding of philosophy in the analytic tradition, which dominates philosophy departments in the Anglophone world.

Paul Roth has recently pleaded for a revival of the "analytical philosophy of history." He questioned "the value of pursuing further literary analyses of narrative" and stated that "*philosophical* discussions focus on normative issues" (Roth 2020: 6, emphasis in the original). Roth has long argued that the narrative structure of historiography is philosophically interesting only to the extent that it is a specific form of explanation, which has to do with its cognitive and semantic aspects (Roth 1988, 1992, 2018, 2020). Since the literary analysis of narrative has nothing to do with the normative issue of evaluating what makes a narrative explanation to be cognitively good or bad, it is not philosophically interesting. Once again, "philosophy" here means a particular kind of philosophy, relating to a specific tradition and so on, which explains some "friction" in certain situations (see Kuukkanen 2014). Like Tucker, Roth proposes an explicit agenda, one which clearly demarcates the meaning of "philosophy of history" and, as such, establishes the criteria by which a given work can be understood as pertaining or not to the field, though we may wonder if and to what extent the agenda is of interest to mainstream analytic philosophers.

Kuukkanen has already perceived a problem that both Tucker and Roth might face in their pleas for a more "philosophical" philosophy of history/historiography. He wrote, "the focus and the scope of the 1960s and 1970s analytic

---

[19] Though he later mentions the "philosophy of historiographic interpretation" as something "closely related to ethics, political philosophy, and aesthetics" (Tucker 2004: 10).

[20] Admittedly, he stated that the philosophy of historiography does examine "the metaphysical assumptions of historiography," but only to the extent that such metaphysical questions can be answered by the study of historiography (Tucker 2001: 52). Nevertheless, others have raised the question over whether it is possible to make such a clear separation and think about historiography without also thinking about the nature of its object – questions that ultimately might not be answerable by recourse to the study of historiography (e.g., Ahlskog 2018: 91–93, Paul 2015a: 10–11).

philosophy of history in this sense would be too narrow in the 21st century. There is too much going on currently and too many alternative avenues of investigation available" (Kuukkanen 2018: 78). Though this is more directly a challenge to Roth's analytical philosophy of history, it can also affect Tucker's philosophy of historiography due to its definitional proximity to the philosophy of science. The catch is precisely in Kuukkanen's awareness that there is a fundamental difference between what he defines as "theory of history" and what philosophers take as "philosophy of history/historiography." As he stated, "it seems to me that it is the theory of history that is booming rather than the philosophy of it. That is, there is an avalanche of studies dealing with the issues of trauma, experience, memory, visual culture, new forms of history-writing, such as even Twitter, etc." (Kuukkanen 2018: 79). These issues that Kuukkanen designates as "theory of history" do not fit neither Tucker's nor Roth's definitions. Whether proposals for a philosophy of historiography or analytical philosophy of history can or want to accommodate these new questions and approaches are important questions for their institutional survival.

2.4 Historians and the "Theory of History"

Ernst Breisach has expressed a widely shared belief among historians when he wrote that "historians, for plausible reasons, have rarely responded with alacrity to opportunities to engage in theoretical debates." In his view, historians "have felt confident about their own complex and sturdy body of epistemological principles and practices (often simply referred to as methodology) – the result of repeated adaptations to and absorptions of rhetorical practices and philosophical propositions over the centuries" (Breisach 2003: 6). This confidence in their ways and "the long-standing suspicions" of philosophy and literary criticism explained the general perception about the historians' "hostility to theory."[21] Historians had *their* theories, that "body of epistemological principles and practices" collectively assembled in direct connection to the needs of actual, practicing historians (see also Klein 2011: 30–32).

Breisach's view is certainly in tune with the disciplinary history of historiography – at least with the versions historians like to write (and read) about themselves. That is, they had a rather long tradition of debating the nature and status of historical knowledge, the beginnings of which can be traced back at least to the German genre of the *Historik*, which combined both epistemological and methodological reflections on the process of

---

[21] For reference, some version of this argument appears in Elton (1967), Marwick (1989, 2001), Zammito (2009). Though he has "remained optimistic," Evans (1999) expressed a less dismissive attitude.

research, source criticism and the like (see Rüsen 1984, 2017, 2020 and Assis 2014). Even in late nineteenth and early twentieth centuries France and Britain, where abstraction and "theorization" were viewed with suspicion, debates over whether history was a science still involved some attempt at grounding historical knowledge (see Torstendahl 2003 and Bentley 2013). As we saw earlier, some philosophers consider these works to be philosophically lacking, to say the least. But this did not seem to bother historians much, confident as they were in their practical expertise (e.g., Zammito 2009). As such, "theory" remained a rather vague term at least until the past few years, and we may wonder if the recent growth of "historical theory" or "theory of history" as areas of interest for historians has helped making the term clearer. Much more common were books on "method," which sometimes included sections dedicated to theoretical questions.

The usage of "historical theory" and "theory of history" among philosophers and historians is almost as confusing as that of "philosophy of history." These phrases too have been victims of the double meaning of the word "history." For instance, both Wolfgang von Leyden (1958) and Patrick Gardiner (1959) have sometimes used "theory of history" and "philosophy of history" interchangeably, ambiguities and all. Once again, the word "history" can refer both to the events that have happened and to our knowledge of them as expressed in (usually) written form.[22] But another layer of confusion is added to the problem due to the word "theory" not having a clear meaning either. In more recent decades, "theory of history" and "historical theory" have been used as umbrellas for many different genres and research agendas, from the various senses of "philosophy of history" to the engagement of historians with literary, social, and political theory, philosophy, anthropology, and so forth (see Jordanova 2011 and Klein 2011). In these cases, the word "theory" can have a variety of meanings, most of which remain unstated. It might mean an explanatory scheme of some phenomenon, or the critical engagement with a given intellectual tradition or author, or even, in some cases, general guidelines that define an activity – and these are only some examples.[23] A "theory of history" in the first of these senses can mean an explanatory scheme for either the totality of events (as in the "substantive" philosophy of history),

---

[22] In some contexts, the word can also mean "the discipline where such knowledge is produced." This third meaning can be particularly important for those who consider this institutional aspect to be important in our theoretical analysis and prefer to distinguish it from the discipline's product (written accounts of past events) and object (the events that happened). See, for instance, Villalobos Álvarez (2017).

[23] When trying to make sense of this wide variety of meanings, I have benefitted from some insightful discussions around social theory and its role in the social sciences (see Abend 2008, Krause 2016, Swedberg 2016, and Bacevic 2018).

a determinate set of those events, or the processes by which we come to know these events (closer to the "critical" philosophy of history). In the second, it can mean the critical engagement with historiography, with texts by or about authors such as Marc Bloch, Eric Hobsbawm, and others. In any case, one can see how even a couple of examples already point us in completely different directions. Furthermore, sometimes the phrases "theory of history" and "historical theory" can have different meanings, and non-native English speakers (myself included) will probably be excused for not capturing the nuances between the two forms.[24]

Back in 2000, François Hartog paraphrased Pierre Chaunu and wrote about the "temptation of epistemology" that some contemporary French historians felt the need to avoid. Hartog's short text is quite telling about the place (or non-place) of theoretical reflection in French historiography, where "problematics and formulations are modulated according to the state of affairs in each major domain of specialties" (Hartog 2000: 82). In the 1970s, three important books had been published by Paul Veyne, Michel Foucault, and Michel de Certeau raising important epistemological issues regarding historical knowledge, as well as questions about the status of professional historiography, but responses were mixed (Foucault 1969, Certeau 1975, Veyne 1978). In the French context, the "critical turn" of the 1980s had been connected to an "identity crisis" and a general perception of disciplinary crisis among historians. As Hartog noted, an effect of this crisis was the coupling of "epistemology" and "historiography" in a reflexive genre that at once historicized historiography itself and questioned its writing.[25] But theoretical reflection understood as epistemology remained under suspicion. Hartog himself remarked that "not all historians have become regular readers of the journal *History and Theory*" (Hartog 2000: 80, emphasis in the original).

Roger Chartier stated it more explicitly when he wrote that philosophical questions about history "seemed without operative relevance for historical practice" (Chartier 1998: 234). In his view, the many problems with how historians talked about "reality" were "without a doubt due to the continuing confusion between a methodological discussion, as old as history, about the value and meaning of the traces that authorize a mediated, indirect knowledge of the phenomena that had produced them, and an epistemological interrogation, generally avoided by historians, maybe because it would paralyze their practice, about the very status of their proclaimed correspondence between their

---

[24] I thank Kleinberg (2021) for alerting me to these nuances.

[25] The journal *Histoire de l'Historiographie/Storia della Storiografia* was launched in this context, in 1982. The manifesto "Pour une histoire de l'historiographie," by Charles-Olivier Carbonell, gives us a sense of how some historians thought about the issue back then (Carbonell 1982).

discourse, their narratives, and the reality that they claim to make comprehensible" (Chartier 1998: 248).[26]

This emphasis on "practical" or "operative" value (or the absence of it) is not entirely unlike that of British and North American historians. After all, contemporary historians are supposed to know that concepts are part and parcel of their work and that the most important developments in twentieth-century historiography came to be precisely due to the disciplinary "friction" between history and its neighboring disciplines – with the social sciences (the first Annales, or German social science history), geography, anthropology (Braudel and the *longue durée*), linguistics, literary theory (New Cultural History), and so on. These exchanges were not always peaceful, sure, but at least they made new empirical approaches to history possible. They had "operative" value. However, any "theory" that had no such practical application remained at best an exotic side interest to many historians in France as well as in other countries.[27]

In 2003, Kevin Passmore, Stefan Berger, and Heiko Feldner framed their textbook for university students as an introduction "to the theoretical ideas – conscious and unconscious that have molded the discipline of history, largely in the West." They claimed that "like it or not, historians cannot avoid theory. ... Even if they do not explicitly use theory themselves, the writing of historians is subtly informed by theoretical assumptions" (Berger, Feldner, and Passmore 2003: xi). But what do the editors mean by "theory" then? They made it clear that theirs was not a textbook about the "philosophy of history" or about "historiography," though they recognized that these aspects too were essential to historians. This explicit distinction is interesting: They mention as pertaining to the philosophy of history issues like "epistemology, causation, the question of whether history is a science or art, of the use of laws in historical explanation" (Berger, Feldner, and Passmore 2003: xi–xii), issues we may connect with what we have seen before about "analytical" or "critical philosophy of history." The editors also claimed that their textbook differed from a manual of historiography (understood as the history of our different ways of knowing about past events) in that it did not "provide a comprehensive survey of the development of the historical profession in its political, social, cultural, and institutional context" (Berger, Feldner, and Passmore 2003: xii). This double distinction is useful for our purposes to the extent that (1) many historians make no distinction between "theory" and "philosophy of history" and, on the other hand, (2)

---

[26] Other examples of a similar attitude include Noiriel (1996) and Charle (2013). Christian Delacroix highlighted the problems with Noiriel position and the "theoretical" versus "practical" dichotomy more broadly – see Delacroix (1997).

[27] About this ambiguous relationship between "historians" and "theory," see Paul and Kleinberg (2018).

many others understand that teaching "theory" equals teaching the history of historiography with an emphasis on "method," as we have just seen. Nevertheless, the editors still frame their task as exploring "the ways in which theory has informed *practical* historical writing" – that is, theory meaning general concepts, explanatory schemes, or approaches that make past events or phenomena intelligible in a certain way. So even when they deal with the intellectual conditions that made professional Western historiography possible, or with some particular approaches to history (such as those of the Annales, or of Marxism, for example), their focus is on the concepts that were involved in each instance.

In his recent textbook, Herman Paul defines historical theory as the "conceptual analysis of *how human beings relate to the past*" (Paul 2015a: 14, emphasis in the original) and justifies the wording choice by appealing to the abandonment of old, superseded dichotomies created by our predecessors. In a sense, then, Paul's historical theory both contains and expands the received definition of philosophy of history in English. On the one hand, it encapsulates the logic and epistemology of historiography that characterized the "critical philosophy of history" as well as the metaphysics of history of the "speculative" branch. On the other, it opens space for addressing other, previously neglected aspects of our relations to the past, such as memory, trauma, intergenerational justice, and so forth.

In a similar vein, Berber Bevernage argued that historical theory should "evolve into a broad 'philosophy of historicities' that, besides focusing on academic historiography, should pay attention to the wide variety of extra-academic ways of dealing with time and historicity" (Bevernage 2012: 117). In his proposal for the future of the field, historical theory involves (1) the recognition that "academic historiography did not develop, and does not function, in an intellectual vacuum but is closely related to a range of particular social, cultural and political assumptions and beliefs about time and historicity on which it is partly dependent but which it can also reinforce or contradict"; that (2) "different approaches to time and historicity have different social, cultural and political functions"; and that (3) "historical discourse can have strong ethical implications" (Bevernage 2012: 117–19).

Both Paul and Bevernage used "historical theory" and "philosophy of history" interchangeably, even appealing to Aviezer Tucker's optimistic assessment of the future of the field. However, as we have seen, Tucker demarcates the philosophy of historiography in very precise ways, a demarcation that is ultimately incompatible with Paul's and Bevernage's wide definitions. Bevernage's complaint that "philosophers of history all too often restrict their perspective to that of philosophy of science and accordingly define the (proper) function of historiography primarily, or even exclusively, in epistemological/ cognitive terms" (Bevernage 2012: 118) seems to miss that this narrow view is entailed by the philosopher's logical treatment of his or her object. It does not mean that historiography is only a cognitive enterprise, but that its cognitive aspect is taken to be its main aspect – or at least the specific aspect in which the philosopher is interested. Moreover, mainstream analytic epistemology has usually rejected claims that such externalities are relevant to our basic cognition.[28] In summary, *this is a feature, not a bug* – and maybe we need to better distinguish "philosophy of history" and "theory of history" after all.

There are, however, more restrictive uses of the phrase. For Nancy Partner, "Historical theory is a coherent yet flexible framework which supports the analysis of historical knowledge and assists our understanding of what kind of knowledge we can have of the past, and precisely how that knowledge is constructed, assembled, and presented" (Partner 2013: 1). Unlike Paul, Partner emphasizes difference and discontinuity between historical theory and the philosophy of history – the former being a "metahistorical frame-work" that "addresses foundational elements of historical knowledge of all times and places," the latter dealing with "the shape and direction of very large scale changes in human collective life over long stretches of time" (Partner 2013: 1–3, *passim*). Earlier, Mary Fulbrook had dedicated her book, *Historical Theory*, to an investigation of "essential issues about the nature of historical knowledge" (Fulbrook 2002: ix). While Partner's and Fulbrook's understanding of historical theory points to an epistemology of historiog-raphy, their usage is closer to the rather long tradition of critical writing by historians themselves – such as Marc Bloch's *Apologie pour l'histoire* (1993),[29] or E. H. Carr's *What is History?* (1987) – which were not merely methodology manuals, but also critical reflections on historical knowledge and the writing of history informed by their professional experiences. In this genre, reflection about historical knowledge might sometimes be called "epistemology" of history but the meaning of "epistemology" here is differ-ent from the standard use in analytic philosophy.

As we have seen, both in the "practical" sense of a discussion about concepts and authors, and in the sense of an "epistemology of history/historiography," "theory of history" or "historical theory" has often been, at best, of marginal

---

[28] For instance, feminist epistemology, standpoint epistemology, and social epistemology faced difficulties in establishing their approaches as valid and relevant in the analytic tradition (see Longino 1990 and 2001, Code 2007, Fricker 2007, Potter 2007, Harding 2015).

[29] Bloch's posthumous publication was first edited and published in 1949 by Lucien Febvre, but later reedited in a more complete and careful manner by Bloch's son, Étienne Bloch, and published in 1993.

interest to historians or, at worst, something they actively reject. Epistemological questions about historical knowledge have tended to focus on whether it was possible reliably to know anything about the past and if so, how. These questions predate modern historiography by centuries, as we can see in Descartes' dismissal of the possibility of reliable historical knowledge or, in Ancient Greece, in Thucydides' criticism of Herodotus. Many of these old themes are recurring in the history of historiography, such as what are the best sources of evidence, how to discern good from bad information, whether impartiality is possible or desirable, and so on. However, analytic philosophers often do not consider these issues to be philosophically interesting. As for the concepts historians use to render their accounts intelligible, historians and social theorists/philosophers have a long history of their own quibbles – in which analytic philosophers might be even less interested.

3 Theory and Philosophy of History Beyond "The West"

In its two usual meanings, history is an important object of thought in former colonial spaces. Faced with the task of making sense of their own realities through the concepts and theories of their colonizers, intellectuals in Asia, Africa, and Latin America were profoundly aware of the dissonances produced by their lack of a place within the Modern European intellectual framework. In the case of history (the flow of events), this meant that the former colonies had to face the challenges of "modernization," of reaching the "civilizational level" of their former European colonizers. From this perspective, their realities could not be seen as more than "imperfect deviations" from the "model" represented by Imperial and Colonial powers such as France and Britain. This also meant adopting the concepts and practices of European "scientific" historiography in an attempt to make sense of their pasts through the intellectual schemes of their colonizers.

Dipesh Chakrabarty expressed it well when he wrote that "faced with the task of analyzing developments or social practices in India, few if any Indian social scientists or social scientists of India would argue seriously with, say, the thirteenth-century logician Gangesa or with the grammarian and linguistic philosopher Bartrihari (first to sixth centuries), or with the tenth- or eleventh-century aesthetician Abhinavagupta" (Chakrabarty 2000: 5). Observations like this one are shared among many of us who were raised outside the "Western World," never fully integrated and never fully humanized. Being always on the outside of the Universal meant that history and historicity (*Geschichtlichkeit*) became crucial aspects of the intellectual labor for postcolonial subjects, whose knowledge was always deemed local and exotic. This is the background of many different attempts at reckoning with the colonial past through a reevaluation of our intellectual structures.[30]

In this section, I have chosen to focus primarily on how Latin American intellectuals have dealt with problems usually associated with the "philosophy of history" and the "theory of history," but the same exercise could very well be done with a focus on other postcolonial contexts, or even on other, more generally non-Western contexts.[31] In fact, I believe it is difficult to ignore the profound implications that works such as those by Gayatri Spivak (1999) or Achille Mbembe (2001) have for our historical thinking – not to mention more direct interventions in the Anglophone theory and philosophy of history, such as those by Chakrabarty (2000) or Sanjay Seth (2004). All these authors raise questions that are fundamental to our philosophical and theoretical understanding of history, from the metaphysics of historical experience to the epistemology of historiography. However, for the sake of brevity, the Latin American case already provides enough relevant evidence for my central claim in this section, which is that, although connected to European and North American intellectual traditions, theorists and philosophers of history outside the Western world have established their own intellectual agendas, and these agendas need to be taken into account if we are to engage critically with fundamental assumptions of European and North American variants of the philosophy of history, theory of history, or historical theory. Rather than merely extending the histories of Western theories and philosophies of history or turning other "local" discussions into exotic variants, I believe it is possible and desirable to promote more frequent exchange. I hope that this stimulates further conversations with other non-Western perspectives as well.

3.1 Overcoming the "Model and Deviation" Framework

Mid- to late-nineteenth and twentieth-century Latin American artists and intellectuals struggled to come to terms with their (post)colonial condition. The very idea of "Latin America," of a shared regional identity, was at the core of many debates (see Mignolo 2006, Altamirano 2008, Beorlegui 2010, Funes 2014). Philosophy of history and scientific (positivist) historiography were often hard

---

[30] A few among many notable examples are Kwasi Wiredu's call for a conceptual decolonization in African philosophy (Wiredu 1998 and 2002), Olúfẹ́mi Táíwò's critical engagement with Hegel's philosophy of history (Táíwò 1998), Achille Mbembe's exploration of the postcolonial condition (Mbembe 2001), and both the Subaltern Studies (Spivak 1999) and Modernity/Coloniality (Castro-Gómez and Grosfoguel 2007) groups.

[31] As the current 2022 events in Ukraine show, large portions of Eastern Europe remain excluded from "the West" by (usually former colonial) powers such as Germany, France, and Britain. That can be extended to other Asian spaces such as China, Korea, and Japan, where colonialism and imperialism have different histories than in "the West." I thank the reviewers for this insight.

to distinguish as these intellectuals established the foundations of their national histories in the mid-1800s. The *Geist* of "the people" as well as the meaning and the general laws of their historical processes were all elements in their attempts at giving their countries and Latin America proper places in history (in the Hegelian sense). And this search for identity took various forms in each of the new countries.

In Mexico, Leopoldo Zea's quest for an authentic Latin American philosophy and his monumental project for the history of ideas in Latin America ran concurrent to Edmundo O'Gorman's challenges to Latin American essentialism and what he saw as the "Rankean" tenets of Mexican historiography in the 1940s (see Zermeño Padilla 2013, Matute 2015, Kotzel 2017, Mora Silva 2018, Franco Neto 2021). In Brazil, the philosophy of history and philosophical history were slowly replaced by "sociological syntheses" that in many ways sought to capture the characteristic features of the nation or to interpret the meanings of its historical process, but better informed by empirical investigations (see Botelho 2010, Nicolazzi 2016). The problems of "origins" and "identity" were also present in Spanish South America, where the local elites struggled to create a new and republican national identity (Maiguashca 2011). In all these cases, knowledge and understanding of the national past were deemed crucial for the task of finding or making a place and a path for the new nations in history.

In 1978, Leopoldo Zea published *Filosofía de la Historia Americana*, a book he described as the "fulfillment of a kind of commitment" to his former teacher, José Gaos. It was part of a large collective project started in the 1940s about the history of ideas in each Latin American country – a project that Gaos considered to be the basis for "la nueva filosofía de la Historia hispanoamericana," the new philosophy of Hispanic American history (Zea 1978: 10–11; see Lizcano Fernández 2004 and Castro-Gómez 2011). Zea and his generation had spent three decades trying to make sense of the relation between Latin American ideas and the general, Universal history of ideas. As Elías Palti wrote, "Zea's contribution was crucial to the development of intellectual history in Latin America as a scholarly discipline. ... Zea was, in fact, the first to approach systematically the particular problems that the writing of history of ideas in the 'periphery' of the West raised; that is, in regions whose cultures have 'a derivative' nature, a term he himself coined" (Palti 2009: 596).

Zea's questions were thus fundamental to his monumental task. Since his history of positivism in Mexico, he kept asking: How could the Mexican positivists be of any relevance to the general history of positivism? Theirs was bound to be either a distorted interpretation of the "real" thing or simply dissolve into universality. "What really mattered was not the

'Latin American contributions' to thought in general, but, on the contrary, its 'failures,' its 'deviations'; in short, the type of 'refractions' that European ideas underwent when they were detached from their original habitat and transplanted to this region," adds Palti (2009: 596). As Latin American philosophers struggled to find their place in history (the flow of events), this interpretive framework of "models" and "deviations" remained a challenge for their historiography. Even the revisionists that targeted Zea, claiming to reframe the history of ideas in Latin America, ultimately failed to escape it (Palti 2009).[32]

In fact, this interpretive framework of "model and deviation" has plagued much of the Latin American intellectual debates in many other disciplines – not only the history of ideas and philosophy, as we have seen with Zea, but also social and political history, economics and economic history, social theory, literary criticism, and so forth (see Palti 2006, Maia 2009). Accordingly, the colonial past has been a fundamental element whenever Latin American intellectuals thought about their realities: Is there a Brazilian, Mexican, or Argentinian essence? An essence to Latin America as a whole? How do art and knowledge produced in Latin America fit the "universal" domain of art and knowledge? Are they bound to be grouped by a geographical or cultural unity, that of "Latin America"? How do we get such unity? In the case of Zea, his project for Latin American philosophy involved the goal of eventually being able to treat it simply as philosophy – "filosofía sin más," as he wrote. Others have disagreed, in his time as in ours (Zea 1969; see Nuccetelli 2020: 234–47). Nevertheless, the question itself has remained relevant, as indicated by its perennial appearance in books and papers by Latin American intellectuals.

There is an important historical-theoretical dimension that cuts across many different disciplines simply by virtue of the question about whether or to what extent one's "being Latin American" is relevant for one's claims to knowledge, or one's artistic expression, for example. This is the clearest in the philosophy of liberation and the Modernity/Coloniality group, with their different critiques of Western modernity. For them, the very foundations of modern Western thought were tainted by the assumption that the modern European white man was the measure of all things, the standard for what could count as universal. From there, philosophers of liberation and those of the Modernity/Coloniality group proposed reevaluations of our intellectual structure based on a critique of Eurocentric conceptions of thought and the search for ways of transcending

---

[32] Palti credits Tulio Halperin Donghi for an approach that superseded, in the 1980s, the whole model and deviation framework for Latin American intellectual history, see Palti (2018a, 2018b).

our intellectual dependence (Cerutti Guldberg 1992, Dussel 1996, Castro-Gómez and Grosfoguel 2007, Castro-Gómez 2011, Walsh and Mignolo 2018; see also Arpini 2010, Vallega 2014, Nuccetelli 2020).

As introduced in Argentina in the 1970s, the philosophy of liberation sought to overcome the "model and deviation" framework by exposing the Eurocentric foundations of modern Western thought. For one of its proponents, Enrique Dussel, Western philosophy's claim to universalism was inseparable from Western colonialism and imperialism: "Modern European philosophers ponder the reality that confronts them; they interpret the periphery from the center. But the colonial philosophers of the periphery gaze at a vision foreign to them, one that is not their own. From the center they see themselves as nonbeing, nothingness" (Dussel 2003: 12). He thus argued that all philosophy, including the Western European kind, is done in concrete historical situations. However, because of European colonialism and imperialism, colonial subjects are denied the possibility of or the capacity for autonomous thinking and, as such, are bound to consume and reproduce what has been thought in the center. It is from this intellectual dependence that Dussel wanted to liberate colonial subjects. Other proponents of the philosophy of liberation have considered Dussel's position to be highly problematic due to his reliance on "a set of uncontaminated first principles" for deriving philosophical truth and his dualistic understanding that equates totality with evil and alterity with good (Schutte 1993: 178–79, see also Cerutti Guldberg 1992: 230–40, 259–64).[33] Though they too rejected the idea that "truth-claims are independent of time, place, history, culture, economics, and so on," their positions diverged from Dussel's version of Heideggerianism and what Horacio Cerutti Guldberg called the "populism of abstract ambiguity" (Schutte 1993: 181–83, Cerutti Guldberg 1992).

More recently, an interdisciplinary group of intellectuals has been advancing a "decolonial turn" in Latin American thought. As with the philosophy of liberation, internal philosophical disagreements make it difficult to characterize a collective agenda, but we can summarize their proposals as a new attempt at understanding and overcoming the Latin American colonial condition of intellectual and material dependence. In a collective volume from 2007, Santiago Castro-Gómez and Ramón Grosfoguel presented the group's ideas and debates by shifting their theoretical framework from the dependence theory to Aníbal Quijano's idea of the "coloniality of power."[34] Central to

---

[33] Dussel has responded to criticisms to his original positions – see, for instance, his chapter in Allen and Mendieta (2021) – but whether he did it successfully or not is up for debate.

[34] Some members of the group published another edited volume, this time in English, a few years later: see Mignolo and Escobar (2010).

their position, the concept of decoloniality described the "transition from Modern colonialism to Global coloniality" (Castro-Gómez and Grosfoguel 2007: 13). They argued that the end of the colonial age and the victory of independence movements had not transformed "the international division of labor between centers and peripheries, neither the ethnic-racial hierarchization of populations" and, therefore, had changed the forms of domination without changing the structure of center–periphery relations. To decolonize then means to address the "racial, ethnic, sexual, epistemic, economic, and gender relations" that survived the twentieth-century end of colonialism (Castro-Gómez and Grosfoguel 2007: 17).

Since then, intellectual divergences have centered around *how* to decolonize. For instance, Catherine Walsh and Walter Mignolo have pushed for "shifting away ... from Western epistemology" and ending "the fictions of modernity" (Walsh and Mignolo 2018: 108–09). In their view, decolonization is tied to "changing the terms (assumptions, regulations) of epistemic, ontological, and economic conversations," that is, "understanding and affirming subjectivities that have been devalued by narratives of modernity" (Walsh and Mignolo 2018: 136 and 146). In contrast, Castro-Gómez has argued that "the biggest error that decolonial theory can make is renouncing to take possession of the political and critical resources offered by modernity itself under the assumption that these resources are in themselves an extension of the logic of capitalism" (Castro-Gómez 2019: 11–12). His idea of decolonization involves "*de-Europeanizing* the legacy of modernity through modernity's own normative criteria," that is, turning the project of modernity against its own Eurocentric assumptions (Castro-Gómez 2019: 11).

Through their struggles with Latin America's postcolonial condition, these diverse intellectual movements engaged in reevaluating the Western foundations of Latin American thought, taking into consideration the particular context of the continent's economic and intellectual dependence and the ubiquity of colonial power structures even in a postcolonial world. Be it in the form of the history of ideas, the philosophy of liberation, or decolonial studies, this task is inevitably tied to questions about the metaphysics of history, the epistemology of historiography, and our moral and political relations to the past. Overcoming the "model-deviation" framework also invites sociological questions around the canonization of texts and authors and the international mobility of intellectuals and ideas, as well as a more general suspicion of claims to universality. Many of the theoretical issues that Latin American historians and theorists of history have raised in the past decades are informed by these broader concerns.

3.2 "The Past is Not Dead," or Theory of History in the Latin American Context

In Latin America, the saying that "the past is not dead" has important connotations. Slavery was fundamental to the discussions around the Latin American colonial legacy, while contemporary historical thought must also deal with the dictatorships that ruled many Latin American countries between the 1960s and the 1990s. Historians, philosophers, social scientists, and other intellectuals have been carefully studying and thinking about what it means to live with the legacy of centuries-long slavery and through decades of violent authoritarian regimes. The idea that the past "is not even past" resonates with the experiences of families that are still haunted by the "disappearance" of their loved ones – mothers, fathers, sisters, brothers, daughters, sons, taken from their homes without notice and never to be seen again. It has also been used by social movements in their struggle for racial and gender equality and against structural forms of racism and sexism. Therefore, it should not surprise us that much of Latin American history and historiography is deeply politicized.

From the mass killings and forced religious conversion of indigenous populations in the sixteenth and seventeenth centuries to the horrors of twentieth-century US-backed coups d'état, the subsequent dictatorships, and state-sponsored violence, a significant part of Latin American history poses difficult challenges to a clear separation between the past and the present, or between what we can know about the past and the existential, moral, or political value of such knowledge. Historiography itself aside, the haunting of the present by the ghosts of slavery and dictatorship is the source of many interesting theoretical works in Latin America (see Sarlo 2005, Altamirano 2008, Cezar 2012, Albuquerque Júnior 2012). In this vein, continental authors such as Michel de Certeau and Walter Benjamin have had an enormous influence over Latin American theoretical engagements with ideas of otherness, violence, oppression, and the sense that thinking about history in/from Latin America involves special attention to relations of power imbalance (see Mendiola 1993, Sebastiani 2011, Nava Murcia 2019, Marcelino 2021).

When our relations to the past are so existentially and politically charged, "theory of history" often acquires a rather engaged tone. For instance, one of the perennial questions for Latin American historians is that of their social role. Of course, that question in itself is not in any way original to the region, but the context of brutal inequality, exclusion, racism, and the living memory of dictatorship gives it an extra sense of urgency. For a while now, Enrique Florescano's *La función social del historiador* has been the locus classicus of the discussion, though much else has been written before and since its original publication in 1994. In his short manifesto, Florescano has argued that the historian is, from the very beginning, "surrounded by inescapable social constraints. On the one hand, he/she is a social product, a result of varied collective currents; on the other, he/she is an individual driven by the desire of overcoming the heritage of the past and renewing his/her craft based on the challenges imposed by his/her present" (Florescano 1997: 64). He then continued by listing and discussing various aspects of this social functioning of history such as the search for identity and the opening toward difference, the attention to continuity and discontinuity, the awareness of the ephemeral character of the world, and so on, leading to the idea, borrowed from Gombrich and Huizinga, that history is ultimately about a society "rendering an account" of what it understands as "its own past." As such, the historian is responsible for delivering the materials for a collective grappling with the past. Others have engaged with the idea, either in Florescano's or in other formulations, with some suggesting that the historian is some sort of curator of historical experiences, and others pointing to debates about the role of historians in public history (see Sánchez León and Izquierdo Martín 2008, Araujo 2018, Nicolazzi 2019).

A related, recent issue concerns the challenges of "denialism." Latin America has not been immune to the recent political context of rising authoritarian movements and new forms of propaganda and misinformation made possible by social media platforms. These have led some historians and theorists of history to reengage in discussions about historical denialism, that is, deliberate practices of misinformation disguised as legitimate dissent in historical interpretation. Though the classical subject remains that of the Holocaust denial and that of other twentieth-century catastrophes, this renewed interest in the falsification of the past has been sparked by a new wave of conflicts around the recent past. More specifically, groups within the military and far-right politicians in Brazil have been denying the practice of torture, assassination, and other atrocities during the Brazilian military dictatorship that lasted from 1964 to 1985, despite the massive evidence and specialized literature that historians have produced to the contrary. Other misinformation strategies include partial or total omission of contradictory known evidence as well as the mischaracterization of existing specialized literature. Beyond doing the usual fact-checking and debunking, historians raised important theoretical and practical questions, such as the challenges both to and from historiographical pluralism, the relation between professional historiography and collective memory, and the political implications of professional historiography (see Bauer and Nicolazzi 2016, Oliveira 2018, Bauer 2019, Avila 2021).

Closely related to those are questions about memory and testimony. As Rodolfo Gamiño Muñoz remarked, "the processes of democratic transition in Latin America marked the memorialist culture in a particular way, which was itself inspired by locally established strategies in the implementation of transitional justice. The memories in the Southern Cone countries (Brazil, Chile, Argentina, Paraguay, Peru and Uruguay) and Central America questioned the global claims of memorialist culture and made it clear that ultimately the contents of memory were connected to social, political, and cultural processes of the nation and locations" (Gamiño Muñoz 2019: 270). As victims of Latin American dictatorships and their families fought for justice, the lines between the truth claims of professional historiography, the experience-grounded testimony of survivors, and the political demands of the living were increasingly blurred. This does not mean that historians relaxed their professional standards and practices – much to the contrary. In Brazil, for instance, their work was openly and widely scrutinized by all the interested parties, most notably by the military and other right-wing reactionary groups, who feared (and often claimed) that these investigations were somehow motivated by a will for "revenge." Dealing with these "difficult pasts" was crucial to a reevaluation of the aims and values of professional historiography in conflicted contexts and, as such, theoretical reflection often pointed to the important and ultimately irresolvable tension between our knowledge of the past and the meanings we attribute to such knowledge in the present. Problems of truth, justice, and ethics came to the foreground as historians and other social scientists tried to find the better ways of navigating the political nuances of their work and dealt with the ethical implications of tapping into the experiences of pain, suffering, anger, and hope of those who were at the receiving end of state-sponsored violence (see Oikión-Solano 2011, Tozzi 2012, Almeida 2018a, Almeida 2018b, Espinosa Moreno 2019).

Hayden White too became an important author for many theorists and philosophers of history. Having proposed that the ways we emplot our histories are contingent on ethical and aesthetical criteria, rather than being given by "the past itself," White assisted historians and theorists of history that were experimenting with the destabilization of our own historical thinking. While many have come to characterize him as the epitome of "postmodernism," here as much as in the Anglophone world, others have decided to engage with his provocations in ways more productive than mere dismissal. His work has been read from many different angles, from concerns with theoretical issues to methodological assistance in the history of historiography (see Tozzi 2009 and 2018, La Greca 2013, Cezar 2015, Avelar 2018, Zermeño Padilla 2020). His late turn to problems of the practical past has also received attention as professional historians have struggled to understand the contemporary shifts in the relation between historiography, collective memory, and public engagement with the past (see Avila 2018, Chinchilla 2020). Among those, one of the most notable is María Inés La Greca's articulation of White's narrativist philosophy of history with Judith Butler's performative theory and Joan Scott's feminist history (La Greca 2014 and 2016). Facing White's pessimism about professional, academic historiography, La Greca makes a significant contribution to our understanding of how professional historiography and broader social demands can be articulated.

3.3 Is There a Non-Western Theory of History?

Having explored a small sample of contemporary theoretical work in Latin America, we see that the adjective "Latin American" adds nothing meaningful to the character of much of what has been published in the past few years on the pages of journals like *História da Historiografia*, *Revista de Teoria da História*, *Historia y Grafía,* and other Latin American journals, either in Portuguese or Spanish. The possible connections between what questions, approaches, and concepts have been privileged in the region and its broader "contexts" are not in any way unique to the non-Western world, in the sense that the concerns of North American, Western European, or Scandinavian theorists and philosophers of history are just as related to their specific historical experiences, to the configuration of their disciplinary fields, or the system of incentives and rewards in the university system, and many other contextual aspects that ultimately have an impact on our research choices. As Kuukkanen noted, memory, trauma, testimony, and many of these themes have been considered relevant to the theory and philosophy of history in other contexts as well. Few, if any of the articles, books, and arguments that I have foregrounded here have their theoretical relevance limited to the geographical location in where they were written. Their scope ranges from the scholarly persona of the engaged historian to articulations between narrativism and feminist theory, through the epistemic, moral, and political issues of testimony – all important issues in themselves.

Latin American theorists and philosophers of history have engaged with a wide variety of authors and themes that we might call "canonical" in the traditional histories of philosophy of history – for instance, *Historia y Grafía* has published a volume dedicated to the work of Arthur Danto as recently as 2017![35] Many of the most important works by White, Danto, or Ankersmit have

---

[35] Matute (2015) brought together some important texts dedicated to the theory and philosophy of history in Mexico in the twentieth century, many engaged at length with continental philosophy of history.

been translated into Spanish thanks to the efforts of groups such as Metahistórias, in Argentina, and some of them have also appeared in Portuguese. Recent contributions to these debates, such as those by Herman Paul, Kalle Pihlainen, and Jouni-Matti Kuukkanen, have also been translated into Spanish and well discussed. As mentioned previously, continental European authors too, such as Michel de Certeau and Walter Benjamin, have been widely read and studied in Mexico, Brazil, Argentina, and Chile – the same regarding the works of Paul Veyne, Michel Foucault, Roland Barthes, Jacques Derrida, and many others. Jörn Rüsen has had a particularly welcoming reception in Brazil due to those working with historical education adopting his concepts, models, and arguments. Much the same could be said for other non-Western contexts.

Some Latin American countries have courses on the "theory of history" as an obligatory component of their curricula for those who choose to graduate in History for their university degree. In Brazil, Argentina, Chile, and Mexico, for instance, these courses are usually titled "teoria da história" (in Portuguese) or "teoría de la historia" (in Spanish) and they mostly deal with the same or very similar contents we discussed in the previous section. Students are introduced to the history of historiography (most often the history of Western European historiography – Germany, France, sometimes Britain) and to basic "theoretical" problems such as historical time, memory, and the writing of history. It is not uncommon that these syllabuses include texts such as *L'écriture de l'histoire*, by Michel de Certeau, something from the volumes of *Faire l'histoire*, and sometimes Reinhart Koselleck and François Hartog appear in discussions about historical time and our relations to the past and the future.[36] Analytic philosophers are usually absent, and even narrativism does not have much of a presence – most commonly, something by White to be read alongside a reply by Carlo Ginzburg or Roger Chartier.[37]

That Latin Americans (and other non-Western intellectuals in general) read, discuss, and build upon canonical figures that come from the "centers" of intellectual production should not be surprising if we consider, with Ana Carolina Barbosa Pereira, that our positioning in the international hierarchy of knowledge production tends to put us in the condition of consumers of "theories of history" produced elsewhere, in places that rank higher in that hierarchy (Pereira 2018). Western authors remain treated as if their thought is somehow more universal than that of their non-Western counterparts when, in fact, their

---

[36] I have studied some of these patterns in more detail in Ohara (2021a).

[37] About this last point, Argentina is a notable exception thanks to the editorial work of Verónica Tozzi Thompson and the Metahistórias group, who championed the translation of Mink, Danto, White, Ankersmit, and many others.

work remains just as contextually bound. However, more than focusing on the contextual grounding of our concepts and categories, I would prefer to insist on the claim that what Latin American (and by extension other non-Western) theorists and philosophers of history have been doing is relevant beyond their direct contexts of production and should be taken into account in any attempt at establishing a common space where researchers that define themselves as working with "theory of history," "historical theory," and "philosophy of history" can engage in a productive dialogue.[38]

4 Toward an Inclusive Definition

As we approach the end of this Element, defining what we mean by the theory and philosophy of history remains a challenging goal. We have seen that the labels "philosophy of history," "theory of history," and "historical theory" have been used to name different, often competing, approaches to the problems of historical knowledge, understanding, meaning, and historicity (*Geschichtlichkeit*). For philosophers, it has not always been clear whether the actual practices of working historians were relevant for their normative inquiries; and even if they were, there remained a question as to whether what historians *said* they were doing was also philosophically relevant. Historians, for their part, remained mostly uninterested in what they saw as the all-too-abstract schemes of the philosophers and were rather skeptical of conceptual discussions that had no immediate practical application in historical research. We may add here that literary theorists sometimes engaged with the problems of historical narrative, but only insofar as it was part of a more general narrative theory, while social theorists were more interested in issues of social or collective memory, and in history as one of many instances of how social groups create and use the/their pasts.

Examples of seemingly irreconcilable interests abound. But despite all the difficulties we have discussed, I believe it might be worth trying and connecting the many different approaches that were developed under the labels of "philosophy of history" and "theory of history" (and other cognates). In fact, I believe this connection is already being made in practice. Nowadays, journals that specialize in issues of the "philosophy of history," "theory of history," and "historical theory" publish texts written by a diverse set of authors from many different intellectual backgrounds: philosophers from both analytical and continental inclinations, historians whose specialties range from intellectual and cultural to social and political history, as well as literary theorists, sociologists,

---

[38] In this sense, I think of my differences with Pereira more in terms of emphasis than in terms of substance, though of course she may disagree with my assessment.

and anthropologists for whose work the historical or temporal dimension is theoretically fundamental. Though no programmatic text or clear definition could possibly account for all those different intellectual agendas, the work that is currently being done suggests that there exists at the very least some "family resemblance" among them.

Of course, no debate has dominated the agenda in the way that the one over historical explanation did for the analytical philosophers of history, but this might be simply because it has become harder for us to ignore other groups, traditions, and approaches like philosophers and historians of yesteryear did. What philosophers of history tend to define as the philosophy of history is but a tiny niche in the broad discipline of philosophy, and something similar can be said about what historians define as the theory of history. Isolated from each other, neither philosophers nor historians will have much of a chance in establishing more robust institutional support for their activities – with the usual symbolic and material consequences. Nevertheless, the journals we read, the seminars we attend, and the networks we participate in have made it so that we have at least a *common space* where we can meet even if there is no *common language* (both literally and figuratively) for us to share. In a sense then, in texts like this Element, we are trying to make sense of something that is already happening, while possibly trying to encourage this or that particular direction.[39] When we discuss what we mean by the labels we use to describe our research interests, we have the opportunity to establish connections over whatever overlap we eventually find. This is the value I see in these discussions.[40]

4.1 The Semantic Aspect of (Sub)Disciplinary Definitions

The (hi)stories and assessments about the trajectory, current state, and future of the field commonly treat some implicit and unclear definition of a given label as referring to a substantive entity (a discipline, for example). It is rather common simply to append the discussions that happen in journals like *History and Theory*, the *Journal of the Philosophy of History*, *Rethinking History*, *Historia y Grafía*, *Historein*, or *História da Historiografia* as a continuation of the "philosophy of history" or of the "theory of history" or "historical theory" without clearly stating what each label means in each context and assuming that "the field" simply exists

---

[39] See, for instance, all the interesting proposals in Paul (2021), Zermeño Padilla (2020), Simon (2019), Ovalle Pastén (2019), Ahlskog (2018), Pereira (2018), Roth (2018), Bouton (2016), Paul (2015b), Kuukkanen (2015), Bevernage et al. (2014), La Greca (2013) – a list not even close to being exhaustive.

[40] Here, I would like to mention a rather informal exchange between Ethan Kleinberg (2021), myself (Ohara 2021b), and Georg Gangl (2021) over the blogs *Geschichtstheorie am Werk*, of Bielefeld University, and the blog of the Centre for Philosophical Studies of History, of the University of Oulu, which can be read on their respective websites.

out there somehow. In these stories that philosophers and historians tell themselves, for instance, narrativism appears either as taking the place of the analytical philosophy of history after the debate over historical explanation had been exhausted or as part of the poststructuralist "attack" on history and the fascination of cultural and intellectual historians with "French theory." I will not discuss the merits and limitations of these emplotments. My point is that framing these stories in this way tends to create unnecessary friction when, for example, it leads to philosophers questioning the "philosophical interest" of questions raised by historians who identify as theorists of history, or to historians raging over the philosophical treatment of their work.

My single divergence from Kuukkanen's otherwise excellent reflections on the Roth–Ankersmit exchange and the current state of "the field" is precisely that he framed the distinction between the philosophy of history and the theory of history as a distinction between substantive entities ("second-order disciplines studying historiography"). He understands the "philosophy of history" as the philosophy of historiography, as Tucker (2004) had proposed, meaning the philosophical analysis of the "practical rationality, problems and concepts" specific to (professional) historiography. In contrast, he wrote of the theory of history that "it is perhaps related to 'philosophy of history', but separate from it nevertheless" – its defining features being "its propensity to take the notions of historiography more or less as they are used by historians and engage in theory building from this starting point" (Kuukkanen 2014: 617; see also Kuukkanen 2021). However, as we have seen, many theorists of history would contest such understanding of the theory of history, claiming that they are engaged in a kind of philosophical analysis of historiography. Are we then to conclude that they are simply naming things wrongly? What if they are indeed engaged in a philosophical analysis of historiography, they are doing philosophy of historiography, rather than theory of history? This does not seem plausible to me, and I have no reason to believe that Kuukkanen would think so. I would rather interpret the substantiation as merely a shorthand and that we know disciplinary definitions are conventional. As such, avoiding that situation is entirely possible by clarifying that the meaning some theorists of history attribute to the label "theory of history" can overlap with the meaning that philosophers of history attribute to the label "philosophy of history" – that is, the philosophical analysis of historiography.[41]

---

[41] Which then invites the question of what historians and philosophers mean by "philosophical analysis," of course, but this would only further clarify the issue. We should also bear in mind that these meanings are related to more fundamental differences between philosophical traditions. The contingent fact that analytic philosophy supposedly dominates the discipline in the Anglophone world should not be relevant to the issue.

We have previously seen that some authors conflate "theory of history" and "historical theory" with the "philosophy of history." Sometimes this issue is related to the use of "philosophy" and "theory" as interchangeable words. This is the case, for example, when "theory" is defined as the "conceptual" study of something – in this case, of history. The previously mentioned text by Chris Lorenz fits this case. To define "theory of history," Lorenz cited Tucker's definition of "philosophy of historiography" (Lorenz 2012: 14). He then stated that "because theory of history consists of the *reflexive discussions* about what the object(s) and language(s) of history – including its method – is and should be, we can expect theory in action when historians define their discipline" (Lorenz 2012: 17, emphasis in the original). This makes it so that all discussions that seek to answer the question "What is history?" and those where historians debate problems of memory, testimony, trauma, and the like are then considered to be part of "theory of history." But the view proposed by Lorenz does not fit into Tucker's definition for the "philosophy of historiography," at least not without stretching its limits and thereby defeating the purpose of Tucker's precise definition.

Similarly, in the *Companion to Historical Theory*, Chiel van den Akker explicitly states that the terms "philosophy of history" and "historical theory" are used interchangeably and defines historical theory broadly as a specialty "concerned with the nature of historical thought, the metaphysics of historical experience, the politics of history-writing, and the intelligibility of the historical process" (van den Akker 2022: xiv). The wide scope of the volume becomes even clearer when we look at its table of contents. The volume's chapters are divided into three main parts: part 1 is titled "Modes and schools of historical thought" and has 12 chapters; part 2 is titled "Epistemology and metaphysics of history" and it too has 12 chapters; and part 3 is titled "Issues and challenges in historical theory," containing 13 chapters. All chapters are well within the limits van den Akker has set, and none is immediately counterintuitive to anyone familiar with the discussions that are framed as "theory of history" or "historical theory" in recent times. However, what the selected chapters show is that, as one would suspect from van den Akker's explicit definition, the scope of "historical theory" here is much wider than what Tucker had defined as "philosophy of historiography." Given that Tucker's definition has been adopted by other philosophers, such as Kuukkanen (2015, 2018), this difference can be significant when we take a broader view of our supposed "field." There is certainly a sense in which the strict definition of "philosophy of historiography" is contained within the scope of "historical theory" as van den Akker defines it, but this is something that needs to be stated and argued rather than assumed.

This wide and encompassing view is in line with Herman Paul's understanding of "historical theory" as a "conceptual analysis of how human beings relate to the past," which seems to include all the aspects van den Akker has listed (Paul 2015a: 14 and 2015b: 4–5). In Paul's *Key Issues in Historical Theory*, we can readily see how this "historical theory" as an analysis of our "relations to the past" can describe much of what theorists of history already do. Paul differentiates between epistemic, moral, political, aesthetic, and material kinds of relations to the past, and leaves open the possibility that the list is not exhaustive (Paul 2015a: 31–32). For the textbook, though, he manages to show how much of what theorists of history have been doing can fit into each of these kinds, and sometimes in more than one: For instance, there is certainly a link to be made between the "political implications" of history writing, part of our political relation to the past, and the questions around the narrative structure of historical thinking and writing, which is part of our aesthetical relation to the past. Their differences are significant enough to justify this separation for the sake of clarity, but where the political ends and the aesthetical begins is never so clear. In Paul's classification, Tucker's philosophy of historiography can fit quite neatly into an inquiry about our cognitive or epistemic relation to the past.

Other authors emplot the history of the "theory of history" or classify its kinds in rather different ways. That has been the case with Jörn Rüsen, for example, who also frequently employs the terms "metahistory" and "theory of history" as synonyms, meaning "an elaborated reflection on the principles of historical thinking" (Rüsen 2020: 92; see also Rüsen 2017: 7 et seq.). Rüsen has positioned his project within the long-running *Historik* tradition, attributing to Chladenius an inaugural role in it. Of particular interest for us is that his retrospective overview of the theory of history extends further into the past than the traditional accounts of the analytical philosophy of history, and it treats the whole debate over historical explanation as a kind of theory of history that has developed mostly in parallel to that of late nineteenth and early twentieth centuries neo-Kantianism (Rüsen 2020: 94–95). Another interesting case is that of Christophe Bouton, who differentiates between continental and Anglo-Saxon branches of philosophy of history when arguing for a Koselleck-inspired "critical theory of history" (Bouton 2016). In his scheme, the continental branch is further divided into speculative and hermeneutic philosophy of history, while the Anglo-Saxon branch is divided into analytical philosophy of history, epistemology of historical knowledge, historical ontology, and global history.

Disagreements about the choice and meaning of each of those terms are expected, and debates about them are important opportunities for exchange as long as the arguments and definitions are explicitly stated. In fact, as I will argue soon, this diversity is salutary for us. However, what must be clear from the beginning is that these disagreements are semantic rather than substantive.[42] "Philosophy of history," "theory of history," and "historical theory" have no nature or essence to which we can refer. Their meanings are dependent on specific disciplinary arrangements, intellectual backgrounds and traditions, and other practical issues. They result from the interaction between participants in the conversation, with all that this entails. In the context of scholarly exchange, these definitions are themselves the object in dispute – that is, there is also a sociological aspect to it. Therefore, rather than ask for the nature of the "philosophy of history," what it *is*, I believe it to be more productive to ask for what the phrase *means* in each context, to clarify these meanings, and to keep in mind that, although neat philosophical definitions can be useful, they will not solve our *dialogue de sourds* unless we get in the habit of recognizing the overlap and connections between our works despite the various labels we use.

4.2 Theory and Theories

Another problem with our lack of attention to the semantic aspect is that those implicit and unclear definitions also come into play in our normative assessment of the "field," however we understand it. Making explicit and clear what we mean by our label of choice is essential to properly justifying the inclusions and exclusions we make in many situations – think of the syllabus of a course or the contents of a companion book. In this sense, what does the word "theory" mean in the phrases "theory of history" and "historical theory"? Again, we might as well begin with work that is already being done under these labels and see if we can parse something out.

As we have seen, the label "theory of history" has come to designate, in both Western and non-Western contexts, studies about memory, testimony, the exclusions and omissions in history-writing, and the reevaluation of fundamental assumptions in historical thought. In some cases, this involves describing the particularly historical relevance of a given philosophical problem (as with testimony, which in "theory of history" is usually about a specific kind of testimony), or inquiring into concepts that have a fundamental role in our acquisition of historical knowledge and understanding (such as the concepts of event, continuity, discontinuity, etc.), or pointing

---

[42] Abend (2008) presents a clear argument for the semantic approach to this issue in the case of the word "theory" among sociologists. I am still not convinced about some of the distinctions Abend made nor about his practical, procedural solution to the matter, but the general case for stating clearly what one understands by "theory" is valuable for my purposes.

to the implications for historiography of theories developed in other disciplines (as in the feminist critique of the history of historiography, or the decolonial critique of our historical-conceptual schemes of understanding). What all these have in common is a kind of "reaching out" of the narrow limits of professional historiography, either for the clarification of concepts, the reevaluation of practices and values, or the borrowing of general ideas. This idea of "theory" as "reaching out" fits well with the general sense of a reflexive, self-critical enterprise that informs how many theorists of history already understand their work. So even if this reflexivity cannot be clearly defined (in the sense of a complete set of operations to be undertaken or conditions to be met), it still implies that theorists of history cross disciplinary boundaries looking for conceptual tools that can help them understand (and possibly propose changes to) our historical thinking and writing (see Betancourt Martínez 2011).

Not all social, literary, critical, feminist, or postcolonial theories are interesting or important to our historical thinking, but some (maybe many) are. In his 1993 textbook on *History and Social Theory*, Peter Burke had already noted that, despite the sometimes tense relationship between historians and social theorists, obtaining historical knowledge would be nearly impossible without concepts, models, or other more or less general theories about the relevant aspects of reality (Burke 1993). That historians borrow ideas and approaches from neighboring disciplines is evident from any historiography manual we currently have – from Ranke's use of philological methods to the most recent fashions of Global, Big, and Deep History, passing through the many varieties of twentieth-century social, economic, and cultural history. In all these cases, ideas, concepts, theories, and methods have been borrowed and adapted from other disciplines, resulting in historians being able to make sense of a greater variety of sources and historical phenomena thereby expanding the field of possibilities of historical knowledge. But this kind of use of theory seems quite unproblematic for "practicing" historians, theorists of history, and philosophers of historiography alike.

Matters get more complicated when we get to other kinds of theoretical enterprises, such as when these "theoretical borrowings" are not directly linked to historiography's cognitive ends, that is, when the reflexive aspect of the "theory of history" is not related to "proper history-writing." Let us go through some examples: Feminist theory has long informed and been reciprocally informed by the writing of women's and, later, gender history. Postcolonial theory too has had a productive reciprocal relationship with postcolonial historiography. I would like to think that no contemporary historian can deny that these interactions have widened the horizons of our historical thinking and that we would be much worse off without all the excellent work that has been done and published on these topics in the past decades. However, there seems to be a continuing resistance to including these "specific" theories in our theory of history courses (Oliveira 2018, Pereira 2018).[43] An element of institutional inertia has certainly a role in this, given that the white, male, Western character of disciplinary canons is not a problem exclusive to historiography (see, e.g., Reed 2006, Tyson 2018). But often one hears: "How is this X theory a theory of history?" In other words, what do social, literary, critical, feminist, or postcolonial theories add to the theory of history? How do these theories relate to the object of the theory of history? All these questions touch on the semantic aspect of the problem that we have discussed earlier: An answer will depend on the meaning that we attribute to the label "theory of history" – but even then, I would argue that these omissions are not justified.

If we consider that by "theory" or "philosophy of history" we mean some restrictive, but clear definition such as "the epistemology of historiography," then we must ask ourselves if these approaches have something to add to the epistemology of historiography. As in our examples, how do gender, race, or geopolitical position relate to our cognition of past events? Do they affect our senses somehow? Are there gendered, racial, or geopolitically influenced experiences of the world? Do they affect our cognitive reasoning and processing of evidence? This is not the place for me to develop a full-fledged argument about my position on a contentious topic, so I will merely indicate that, although mainstream analytic epistemology rejects this idea, there are philosophers even within the analytic tradition that differ from such a position (e.g., in standpoint epistemology, feminist philosophy of science). If we also consider the continental tradition, then the answer is even less obvious. Therefore, we should at least approach with an open mind the matter of, as in our example, whether gender, race, and geopolitical position are related to our cognitive processes in ways relevant to historical thinking and knowledge.

Alternatively, if we mean by "theory" or "philosophy of history" something broader, such as the reflexive, self-critical practice in which we examine the conceptual structure of our historical thinking, including the practices of professional historiography, then we must ask ourselves about

---

[43] I am referring here to Brazil, one of the few places where theory courses are mandatory for undergraduate and graduate history students. Of course, given that theory courses themselves are not commonly mandatory – and often do not even exist – in other places, this only compounds the issue.

what these theories can help us understand about the wide variety of ways we engage in historical thinking. For instance, the gendered character of certain historiographical practices, such as the nineteenth-century seminar or the disciplinary histories of historiography, has been well documented and studied in the past decades (see Scott 1988, Smith 2000, Smith 2006, Cabrera Gómez and Errázuriz Tagle 2015, Liblik 2015, Erbereli Jr 2016, Oliveira 2018, Machado 2021 – the list could go on). Race has also been crucial in the profession – not only in terms of the social structure of the discipline but also in assessments of epistemic value (see White 2008, Trapp 2019, Miranda and Assunção 2021). Since the empirical evidence we have points to these being relevant factors in the actual structure of professional historiography as well as in our research practices, we are well justified in asking both further empirical questions and theoretical ones. If women, people of color, and many other social groups were excluded both as subjects and as authors of the histories we know, or if the language by which we refer to virtuous or vicious cognitive traits has gendered connotations, we might as well investigate whether, how, and to what extent such exclusions affected our cognitive practices. We might also think about the political and existential aspects of our memory culture or the social arrangements that make certain groups more or less likely to engage in professional historical research. All these are legitimate and important questions for the "theory of history" in a broader sense, one that is close to much of the work that is being done under such a label. And for these questions, social, literary, feminist, postcolonial, and other theories can be of great benefit to us. Whether a given "theory" is relevant as a "theory of history" has less to do with its disciplinary origins, preferred object, or particular approach than with whether it can assist us in dealing with the theoretical problems that our own definitions of "theory of history" established as valid.

4.3 A Broad Understanding of "Theory and Philosophy of History"

Both Herman Paul (2021) and Zoltán Simon (2019) have recently argued for labels with broad and inclusive meanings. Pointing to the experience in the History and Philosophy of Science, Paul has proposed that we think of a "hermeneutic space" where historians and philosophers of history can engage each other's ideas in an open-ended conversation, a space he called the History and Philosophy of History (HPH). As the "hermeneutic" adjective suggests, this space does away with the need for previously agreed concepts, approaches, or questions, or a well-defined research agenda. Instead, "the only demand that this space makes upon participants is that they are, and remain, committed to dialogical virtues (curiosity, generosity, empathy, open-mindedness) without which no productive exchange can take place" (Paul 2021: 176). Furthermore, the proposal for HPH does not involve redefining more specific terms such as "theory of history" or "philosophy of history." Rather, it merely signals that dialogue and exchange among these are possible, that they are encouraged, and that new ideas might emerge from this dynamic. Paul's proposal is good, even if he recognizes that the experience of the History and Philosophy of Science has had its practical problems. Its main advantage is not demanding a general reorientation of the field nor necessarily a change in how current researchers understand their own work. All we need would be to invest in widening the spaces where these exchanges already happen.

For Simon, our current challenge involves a generational shift in which the categories that organized the work of our predecessors fail to account for the questions we currently ask. By framing his assessment of the situation under a broad understanding of "theory and philosophy of history," one that "somehow encompasses all the different understandings of 'theory,' 'philosophy,' and 'history'" (Simon 2019: 56), he considers two senses in which the phrase "theory of history" has been used in current debates: "a theory that belongs to history as historical studies and constitutes a specific method or approach, and a theory about the entirety of history understood either as historical studies or the changing world of human affairs (or a theory about both)" (Simon 2019: 64). Like Paul's proposal for HPH, Simon's does not involve a redefinition of specific terms but rather envisions a broad and inclusive space for exchange and collaboration. His distinction between theories "that belong to history" and theories "about history" indeed clearly defines the scope of each one without resorting to an artificial (and still unclear) separation between the epistemology of historiography and the metaphysics of history.

I borrow from Simon the idea of a broad, inclusive understanding of a unified label, "theory and philosophy of history," one which does not preclude the possibility of defining more specific agendas, such as Tucker's definition for the philosophy of historiography, Eugenia Gay's aesthetic theory of history, Roth's plea for reviving analytic philosophy of history, Kleinberg's theory of history polyphonic, Ahlskog's Collingwoodian philosophy of history, Bouton's critical theory of history, La Greca's narrativist and performative philosophy of history, and so on. The proliferation of agendas, themes, and traditions is salutary rather than deleterious for us. As current research shows, our modes of relating to the past(s) are multiple and, in many ways, interconnected. When it comes to (human) history, cognition is not always easily disentangled from cultural contingencies and all the other ways we relate to the past. Therefore, we need a wide variety of approaches to understand what these modes are, how they work, and how they are sometimes entangled in certain situations.

Here, we might as well follow Kuukkanen's advice for the philosophy of historiography, even if we mean by theory and philosophy of history something different than what he had in mind. He wrote, "[T]he philosophy of historiography should be both attentive and open to new problems, turns and discussions. The philosophy of historiography should not tie itself to any specific philosophical school or tradition. That is, it is not possible to define the scope of an entire field of investigation from a perspective of any one specific tradition, no matter whether it is Gadamerian, positivistic, Quinean, Whitean, postmodernist, narrativist or something else" (Kuukkanen 2018: 79). Open-mindedness and generosity will be fundamental for any wide-ranging project for our field – be it Paul's HPH, Simon's or my idea of "theory and philosophy of history," or even Kuukkanen's view of distinct but closely related fields. Thus, I borrow from Herman Paul the idea of establishing a hermeneutic space, where historians, philosophers, and other researchers interested in our relations to the past(s) can discuss their issues and hopefully engage in respectful and creative exchanges.

Finally, I also believe that this broad understanding of "theory and philosophy of history" is merely naming something that is already taking place on the pages of our specialized journals and in our events. The conflation of the phrases "philosophy of history," "philosophy of historiography," "historical theory," and "theory of history" indicates that our intellectual communities perceive there to be more continuity than discontinuity between each of our rather narrow niches. What can usually be taken as a lack of clarity is, in this interpretation, evidence that we already believe that we share common questions, issues, and references – even if only partially and imperfectly. This does not mean that discussing and trying to make sense of our current situation is pointless. On the contrary, these discussions have at least the benefit of making clear what we mean by the names we give to our field(s) – which, given the confusion we have seen, is already an important and valuable result in itself. But most importantly, by making sense of our current situation and knowing what exchanges are already happening, we can work more effectively in the direction of institutional recognition and further incentivize collaboration across disciplines, intellectual traditions, and linguistic borders. Given that what we are trying to understand is already taking place, to discuss "the field" is also, in a sense, to make it. I hope that my proposal for a broad understanding of the theory and philosophy of history can help us with building this common space, even if it still cannot provide us with a common language.

References

Abend, Gabriel (2008). The Meaning of "Theory." *Sociological Theory* 26 (2): 173–99.

Ahlskog, Jonas (2018). The Idea of a Philosophy of History. *Rethinking History* 22 (1): 86–104.

Albuquerque Júnior, Durval Muniz de (2012). As Sombras Brancas: Trauma, Esquecimento e Usos do Passado. In Flávia Varella et al., eds., *Tempo Presente & Usos do Passado*, Rio de Janeiro: Editora FGV, pp. 51–66.

Allen, Amy and Mendieta, Eduardo, eds. (2021). *Decolonizing Ethics: The Critical Theory of Enrique Dussel*, Pennsylvania: The Pennsylvania State University Press.

Almeida, Gisele Iecker de (2018). Undoing Brazil's Dictatorial Past. In Natascha Mueller-Hirth and Sandra Rios Oyola, eds., *Time and Temporality in Transitional and Post-Conflict Societies*, London: Routledge, pp.143–60.

Altamirano, Carlos (2008). Pasado Presente. In Clara E. Lida, Horacio Crespo, and Pablo Yankelevich, eds., *Argentina, 1976. Estudios en Torno al Golpe de Estado*, México: El Colegio de México; Fondo de Cultura Económica, pp. 17–33.

Ankersmit, Frank R. (1983). *Narrative Logic: A Semantic Analysis of the Historian's Language*, The Hague: Martinus Nijhoff.

Ankersmit, Frank R. (1986). The Dilemma of Contemporary Anglo-Saxon Philosophy of History. *History and Theory* 25 (4), 1–27.

Ankersmit, Frank R. (1994). *History and Tropology: The Rise and Fall of Metaphor*, Berkeley: University of California Press.

Ankersmit, Frank R. (2001). *Historical Representation*, Stanford: Stanford University Press.

Ankersmit, Frank R. (2012). *Meaning, Truth, and Reference in Historical Representation*, Leuven: Leuven University Press.

Ankersmit, Frank R., Domańska, Ewa and Kellner, Hans, eds. (2009). *Re-Figuring Hayden White*, Stanford: Stanford University Press.

Araujo, Valdei Lopes de (2011). Sobre a Permanência da Expressão Historia Magistra Vitae no Século XIX Brasileiro. In Fernando Nicolazzi, Helena Mollo, and Valdei Lopes de Araujo, eds., *Aprender com a História? O Passado e o Futuro de uma Questão*, Rio de Janeiro: Editora FGV, pp. 131–47.

Araujo, Valdei Lopes de (2018). O Direito à História: O(a) Historiador(a) como Curador(a) de uma Experiência Histórica Socialmente Distribuída. In Rodrigo Perez, Géssica Guimarães, and Leonardo Bruno, eds., *Conversas sobre o Brasil: Ensaios de Crítica Histórica*, Rio de Janeiro: Autografia, pp. 191–216.

Arpini, Adriana (2010). Filosofía y Política en el Surgimiento de la Filosofía Latinoamericana de la Liberación. *Solar* 6: 125–49.

Assis, Arthur Alfaix (2014). *What Is History For? Johann Gustav Droysen and the Functions of Historiography*, New York: Berghahn Books.

Avelar, Alexandre de Sá (2018). Hayden White nas Páginas de History and Theory. Dois momentos: 1980 e 1998. *ArtCultura* 20 (37): 37–49.

Avila, Arthur Lima de (2018). Indisciplinando a Historiografia: Do Passado Histórico ao Passado Prático, da Crise à Crítica. *Revista Maracanan* 18: 35–49.

Avila, Arthur Lima de (2021). Qual passado escolher? Uma discussão sobre o negacionismo histórico e o pluralismo historiográfico. *Revista Brasileira de História* 42 (87): 161–84.

Bacevic, Jana (2018). What Is Social Theory? In *Social Theory Applied*, Glasgow, last accessed on January 25, 2022, https://socialtheoryapplied .com/2018/06/28/what-is-social-theory-interview-with-jana-bacevic/.

Bann, Stephen (1984). *The Clothing of Clio: A Study of the Representation of History in Nineteenth-Century Britain and France*, Cambridge: Cambridge University Press.

Bauer, Caroline Silveira (2019). La dictadura cívico-militar brasileña en los discursos de Jair Bolsonaro: usos del pasado y negacionismo. *Relaciones Internacionales* 57: 37–51.

Bauer, Caroline Silveira and Nicolazzi, Fernando (2016). O Historiador e o Falsário: usos públicos do passado e alguns marcos da cultura histórica contemporânea. *Varia Historia* 32 (60): 807–35.

Bentley, Michael (2013). The Turn Towards "Science": Historians Delivering Untheorized Truth. In Nancy Partner and Sarah Foot, eds., *The SAGE Handbook of Historical Theory*, Los Angeles: SAGE, pp. 10–22.

Beorlegui, Carlos (2010). *Historia del Pensamiento Filosófico Latinoamericano: Una Búsqueda Incesante de la Identidad*, 3rd ed., Bilbao: Universidad de Deusto.

Berger, Stefan, Feldner, Heiko, and Passmore, Kevin, eds. (2003). *Writing History: Theory & Practice*, London: Arnold.

Bernheim, Ernst (1908). *Lehrbuch der Historischen Methode und der Geschichtsphilosophie*, Leipzig: Verlag von Duncker & Humblot.

Betancourt Martínez, Fernando (2011). ¿Por qué es necesaria la investigación en teoría de la historia? *Históricas* 90: 16–23.

Bevernage, Berber (2012). From Philosophy of History to Philosophy of Historicities: Some Ideas on a Potential Future of Historical Theory. *BMGN – Low Countries Historical Review* 127 (4): 113–20.

Bevernage, Berber, Delanote, Broos, Froeyman, Anton, and Van De Mieroop, Kenan (2014). Introduction: The Future of the Theory and Philosophy of History. *Journal of the Philosophy of History* 8 (2): 141–48.

Bevernage, Berber et al. (2019). Philosophy of History after 1945: A Bibliometric Study. *History and Theory* 58 (3): 406–36.

Bird, Alexander (2015). Kuhn and the Historiography of Science. In William J. Devlin and Alisa Bokulich, eds., *Kuhn's Structure of Scientific Revolutions – 50 Years On*, Cham: Springer, pp. 23–38.

Blanke, Horst Walter, Fleischer, Dirk and Rüsen, Jörn (1984). Theory of History in Historical Lectures: The German Tradition of Historik, 1750–1900. *History and Theory* 23 (3): 331–56.

Bloch, Marc (1993). *Apologie pour l'histoire ou métier d'historien*, édition critique préparée par Étienne Bloch, Paris: Armand Colin.

Bos, Jacques (2018). Ankersmit's Dutch Writings and Their Audience. *Journal of the Philosophy of History* 12 (3): 450–71.

Botelho, André (2010). Passado e Futuro das Interpretações do País. *Tempo Social* 22 (1): 47–66.

Bouton, Christophe (2016). The Critical Theory of History: Rethinking the Philosophy of History in the Light of Koselleck's Work. *History and Theory* 55 (2): 163–84.

Breisach, Ernst (2003). *On the Future of History: The Postmodernist Challenge and Its Aftermath*, Chicago: The University of Chicago Press.

Brzechczyn, Krzysztof, ed. (2018). *Towards a Revival of Analytical Philosophy of History: Around Paul A. Roth's Vision of Historical Sciences*. Leiden: Brill-Rodopi.

Burke, Peter (1993). *History and Social Theory*, Ithaca: Cornell University Press.

Cabrera Gómez, María Josefina and Errázuris Tagle, Javiera (2015). Historia, Mujeres y Género en Chile: La Irrupción de las Autoras Femininas en las Revistas Académicas. Los Casos de Revista Historia y Cuadernos de Historia. *Historia* 48 (1): 279–99.

Canhada, Julio (2020). *O Discurso e a História: A Filosofia no Brasil no Século XIX*, São Paulo: Edições Loyola.

Carbonell, Charles-Olivier (1982). Pour une histoire de l'historiographie. *Storia della Storiografia* 1: 7–25.

Carr, David (1991). *Time, Narrative, and History*, Bloomington: Indiana University Press.

Carr, Edward H. (1987). *What is History?*, 2nd ed., London: Penguin Books.

Carrard, Philippe (2017). *History as a Kind of Writing: Textual Strategies in Contemporary French Historiography*, Chicago: The University of Chicago Press.

Carrard, Philippe (2018). Hayden White and/in France: Receptions, Translations, Questions. *Rethinking History* 22 (4): 581–97.

Cassirer, Ernst (1950). *The Problem of Knowledge: Philosophy, Science, and History since Hegel*, transl. William H. Woglom and Charles W. Hendel, New Haven: Yale University Press.

Castro-Gómez, Santiago (2011). *Crítica de la Razón Latinoamericana*, 2nd ed., Bogotá: Editorial Pontificia Universidad Javeriana.

Castro-Gómez, Santiago (2019). *El Tonto y los Canallas: Notas para un Republicanismo Transmoderno*, Bogotá: Pontificia Universidad Javeriana.

Castro-Gómez, Santiago and Grosfoguel, Ramón, eds. (2007). *El Giro Decolonial: Reflexiones para una Diversidad Epistémica Más Allá del Capitalismo Global*, Bogotá: Siglo del Hombre Editores.

Certeau, Michel de (1975). *L'Écriture de l'Histoire*, Paris: Gallimard.

Cerutti Guldberg, Horacio (1992). *Filosofía de la Liberación Latinoamericana*, 2nd ed., México: Fondo de Cultura Económica.

Cezar, Temístocles (2012). Tempo Presente e Usos do Passado. In Flávia Varella et al., eds., *Tempo Presente & Usos do Passado*, Rio de Janeiro: Editora FGV, pp. 31–49.

Cezar, Temístocles (2015). Hamlet Brasileiro: ensaio sobre giro linguístico e indeterminação historiográfica (1970–1980). *História da Historiografia* 8 (17): 440–61.

Chakrabarty, Dipesh (2000). *Provincializing Europe: Postcolonial Thought and Historical Difference*. Princeton: Princeton University Press.

Charle, Christophe (2013). *Homo Historicus : Réflexions sur l'histoire, les historiens et les sciences sociales*, Paris: Armand Colin.

Chartier, Roger (1997). *On the Edge of the Cliff: History, Language, and Practices*, translated by Lydia G. Cochrane, Baltimore: The Johns Hopkins University Press.

Chartier, Roger (1998). *Au Bord de la Falaise : L'Histoire entre Certitudes et Inquiétude*, Paris: Albin Michel.

Chinchila, Perla (2020). La Historia magistra vitae y el practical past. *Historia y Grafía* 55: 83–127.

Clark, Anna, Berger, Stefan, Hughes-Warrington, Marnie, and Macintyre, Stuart (2018). What is History? Historiography Roundtable. *Rethinking History* 22 (4): 500–24.

Code, Lorraine (2007). Feminist Epistemologies and Women's Lives. In Linda Martín Alcoff and Eva Feder Kittay, eds., *The Blackwell Guide to Feminist Philosophy*, Malden: Blackwell, pp. 211–34.

Collingwood, Robin G. (1946). *The Idea of History*, Oxford: The Clarendon Press.

Danto, Arthur C. (1962). Narrative Sentences. *History and Theory* 2 (2): 146–79.

Danto, Arthur C. (1995). The Decline and Fall of the Analytical Philosophy of History. In Hans Kellner and Frank R. Ankersmit, eds., *A New Philosophy of History*, London: Reaktion Books, pp. 70–85.

Delacroix, Christian (1997). Histoire : Le syndrome épistémologique. *Espace Temps* 64–65: 63–68.

Domańska, Ewa (1998). *Encounters: Philosophy of History after Postmodernism*, Charlottesville: University Press of Virginia.

Domańska, Ewa and María Inés La Greca, eds. (2019). Globalizing Hayden White. *Rethinking History* 23 (4): 533–81.

D'Oro, Giuseppina (2008). The Ontological Backlash: Why Did Mainstream Analytic Philosophy Lose Interest in the Philosophy of History? *Philosophia* 36 (4): 403–15.

Dray, William H. (1954). Explanatory Narrative in History. *The Philosophical Quarterly* 4 (14): 15–27.

Dray, William H. (1957). *Laws and Explanation in History*, Oxford: Oxford University Press.

Dray, William H. (1964). *Philosophy of History*, Englewood Cliffs: Prentice-Hall.

Dray, William H., ed. (1966). *Philosophical Analysis and History*, New York: Harper & Row.

Dray, William H. (1989). Narrative and Historical Realism. In William H. Dray, ed., *On History and Philosophers of History*, Leiden: Brill, pp. 131–63.

Droysen, Johann Gustav (1893). *Principles of History*, Boston: Ginn.

Dussel, Enrique (1992). El Proyecto de una Filosofía de la Historia Latinoamericana. *Cuadernos Americanos* 35: 203–18.

Dussel, Enrique (1996). *Filosofía de la Liberación*, 4th ed., Bogotá: Editorial Nueva America.

Dussel, Enrique (2003). *Philosophy of Liberation*, transl. Arquilina Mertinez and Christine Morkovsky, Eugene: Wipf & Stock.

Elton, G. R. (1967). *The Practice of History*, New York: Thomas Y. Crowell.

Erbereli Jr., Otávio (2016). De Preterida a Preferida: Considerações em torno da Trajetória Intelectual de Alice Piffer Canabrava (1935–1951). *História da Historiografia* 9 (22): 97–115.

Espinosa Moreno, Fernanda (2019). El surgimiento público de la víctima en Colombia: la voz testimonial de la tortura (1978–1979). *Historia y Grafía* 52: 129–56.

Evans, Richard J. (1999). *In Defense of History*, New York: W. W. Norton.

Florescano, Enrique (1997). *La Historia y el Historiador*, México: Fondo de Cultura Económica.

Foucault, Michel (1969). *L'Archéologie du Savoir*, Paris: Gallimard.

Franco Neto, Mauro (2021). As Armadilhas do Ser: História, Vida e uma Resposta Ontológica à Filosofia do Ser Nacional. *Revista de Teoria da História* 24 (1): 104–25.

Franzini, Fábio (2017). Mr. White chega aos trópicos: notas sobre Meta-História e a recepção de Hayden White no Brasil. In Julio Bentivoglio e Verónica Tozzi, eds., *Do Passado Histórico ao Passado Prático: 40 anos de Meta História*, Serra: Milfontes, pp. 329–43.

Fricker, Miranda (2007). *Epistemic Injustice: Power & the Ethics of Knowing*, Oxford: Oxford University Press.

Friedländer, Saul, ed., (1992). *Probing the Limits of Representation: Nazism and the "Final Solution"*, Cambridge, MA: Harvard University Press.

Fulbrook, Mary (2002). *Historical Theory*, London: Routledge.

Funes, Patricia (2014). *Historia Mínima de las Ideas Políticas en América Latina*. Mexico: El Colegio de Mexico.

Gallie, Walter B. (1963). The Historical Understanding. *History and Theory* 3 (2): 149–202.

Gallie, Walter B. (1964). *Philosophy and the Historical Understanding*, New York: Schocken Books.

Gamiño Muñoz, Rodolfo (2019). Memorias de la Violencia Política en América Latina: Tensiones y Complementaridades. *Historia y Grafía* 52: 267–99.

Gangl, Georg (2021). Facing the Music. In *Philosophy of History Now*, Oulu, accessed on January 3, 2022, www.oulu.fi/blogs/facingthemusic.

Gardiner, Patrick (1952). *The Nature of Historical Explanation*, Oxford: The Clarendon Press.

Gardiner, Patrick, ed. (1959). *Theories of History*, Glencoe: The Free Press.

Gardiner, Patrick, ed. (1974). *The Philosophy of History*, Oxford: Oxford University Press.

Gay, Eugenia (2020). Una verdad estética para la teoría de la historia. *Anuario de la Escuela de Historia* 32: 1–29.

Geyl, Pieter, Arnold J. Toynbee, and Pitirim A. Sorokin (1949). *The Pattern of the Past: Can We Determine It?* Boston: The Beacon Press.

Goggin, Jacqueline (1992). Challenging Sexual Discrimination in the Historical Profession: Women Historians and the American Historical Association, 1890–1940. *The American Historical Review* 97 (3): 769–802.

Goldstein, Leon J. (1976). *Historical Knowing*, Austin: University of Texas Press.

Goldstein, Leon J. (1996). *The What and the Why of History: Philosophical Essays*, Leiden: E. J. Brill.

Gorman, Jonathan (2009). *Historical Judgement: The Limits of Historiographical Choice*, Montreal: McGill-Queen's University Press.

Gorman, Jonathan (2018). Traditions in Philosophy of History. *Maynooth Philosophical Papers* 9: 59–79.

Gorman, Jonathan (2021). Encompassing the Future. In Jouni-Matti Kuukkanen, ed., *Philosophy of History: Twenty-First-Century Perspectives*, London: Bloomsbury Academic, pp. 23–43.

Grever, Maria and Stuurman, Siep, eds. (2007). *Beyond the Canon: History for the Twenty-first Century*, Basingstoke: Palgrave Macmillan.

Guimarães, Manoel Luiz Salgado (2011). *Historiografia e Nação no Brasil: 1838–1857*, Rio de Janeiro: EdUERJ.

Harding, Sandra (2015). *Objectivity and Diversity: Another Logic of Scientific Research*, Chicago: The University of Chicago Press.

Harlan, David (1997). *The Degradation of American History*, Chicago: The University of Chicago Press.

Hartog, François (2000). La Tentation de l'Épistémologie ? *Le Débat* 112 (5): 80–83.

Hempel, Carl (1942). The Function of General Laws in History. *The Journal of Philosophy* 39 (2): 35–48.

Hook, Sidney, ed. (1963). *Philosophy and History: A Symposium*, New York: New York University Press.

Jordanova, Ludmilla (2011). What's in a Name? Historians and Theory. *English Historical Review* 126 (523): 1456–77.

Kansteiner, Wulf (1993). Hayden White's Critique of the Writing of History. *History and Theory* 32 (3): 273–95.

Kansteiner, Wulf (2009). Success, Truth, and Modernism in Holocaust Historiography: Reading Saul Friedländer Thirty-Five Years After the Publication of Metahistory. *History and Theory* 47 (4): 25–53.

Kellner, Hans (1989). *Language and Historical Representation: Getting the Story Crooked*, Madison: University of Wisconsin Press.

Kellner, Hans and Ankersmit, Frank R., eds. (1995). *A New Philosophy of History*, London: Reaktion Books.

Klein, Kerwin Lee (2011). *From History to Theory*. Berkeley: University of California Press.

Kleinberg, Ethan (2021). Reflections on Theory of History Polyphonic. In *Geschichtstheorie am Werk*, Bielefeld, accessed on January 3, 2002, https://gtw.hypotheses.org/757.

Kotzel, Andrés (2017). *La Idea de América en el Historicismo Mexicano: José Gaos, Edmundo O'Gorman y Leopoldo Zea*, 2nd ed., Buenos Aires: TeseoPress.

Kramer, Lloyd S. (1989). Literature, Criticism, and Historical Imagination: The Literary Challenge of Hayden White and Dominick LaCapra. In Lynn Hunt, ed., *The New Cultural History*, Berkeley: University of California Press, pp. 97–128.

Krause, Monika (2016). The Meanings of Theorizing. *The British Journal of Sociology* 67 (1): 23–29.

Kuukkanen, Jouni-Matti (2014). The Current State of Play in the Theory and Philosophy of History: The Roth–Ankersmit Controversy and Beyond. *Rethinking History* 18 (4): 613–19.

Kuukkanen, Jouni-Matti (2015). *Postnarrativist Philosophy of Historiography*. Basingstoke: Palgrave Macmillan.

Kuukkanen, Jouni-Matti (2018). The Future of Philosophy of Historiography. In Krzysztof Brzechczyn, ed., *Towards a Revival of Analytical Philosophy of History: Around Paul A. Roth's Vision of Historical Sciences*. Leiden: Brill-Rodopi, pp. 73–94.

Kuukkanen, Jouni-Matti (2021). A Conceptual Map for Twenty-First-Century Philosophy of History. In Jouni-Matti Kuukkanen, ed., *Philosophy of History: Twenty-First-Century Perspectives*, London: Bloomsbury Academic, pp. 1–19.

La Greca, María Inés (2013). Entre la Ironía y el Romance: Pasado, Presente y Futuro de la Filosofía de la Historia Narrativista. *Páginas de Filosofía* XIV (17): 22–48.

La Greca, María Inés (2014). Narrative Trouble, or Hayden White's Desire for a Progressive Historiography Refigured by Judith Butler's Performativity Theory. *Storia Della Storiografia* 65 (1): 117–29.

La Greca, María Inés (2016). Hayden White and Joan W. Scott's Feminist History: The Practical Past, the Political Present and an Open Future. *Rethinking History* 20 (3): 395–413.

Langlois, Charles-Victor and Seignobos, Charles (1898). *Introduction aux Études Historiques*, Paris: Librairie Hachette.

Larvor, Brendan (2000). History, Role in the Philosophy of Science. In W. H. Newton-Smith, ed., *A Companion to the Philosophy of Science*, Malden: Blackwell, pp. 154–61.

Liblik, Marmem Silvia da Fonseca Kummer (2015). A Formação e a Profissionalização de Historiadoras Universitárias Brasileiras (1960–1980). *História Oral* 18 (2): 7–34.

Little, Daniel (2010). *New Contributions to the Philosophy of History*, Dordrecht: Springer Netherlands.

Lizcano Fernández, Francisco (2004). *Leopoldo Zea: Una Filosofía de la Historia*, 2nd ed., México: Universidad Nacional Autónoma de México.

Longino, Helen (1990). *Science as Social Knowledge: Values and Objectivity in Scientific Inquiry*, Princeton: Princeton University Press.

Longino, Helen (2001). *The Fate of Knowledge*, Princeton: Princeton University Press.

Lorenz, Chris (1998). Can Histories Be True? Narrativism, Positivism, and the "Metaphorical Turn." *History and Theory* 37 (3): 309–29.

Lorenz, Chris (2012). History and Theory. In Axel Schneider & Daniel Woolf, eds., *The Oxford History of Historical Writing: Volume 5: Historical Writing since 1945*, Oxford: Oxford University Press, pp. 13–35.

Machado, Daiane (2021). Um Perfil da História Disciplinar: Carreira Acadêmica e Poder Masculino no Arquivo Pessoal da Historiadora Adeline Daumard. *História da Historiografia* 14 (36): 289–318.

Maia, João Marcelo (2009). Pensamento Brasileiro e Teoria Social: Notas para uma Agenda de Pesquisa. *Revista Brasileira de Ciências Sociais* 24 (71): 155–96.

Maiguashca, Juan (2011). Historians in Spanish South America: Cross-References between Centre and Periphery. In Stuart Macintyre, Juan Maiguashca and Attila Pók, eds., *The Oxford History of Historical Writing: 1800–1945*. Vol. IV in *The Oxford History of Historical Writing*. Oxford: Oxford University Press, pp. 463–87.

Mandelbaum, Maurice (1967) [1938]. *The Problem of Historical Knowledge*, New York: Harper Torchbooks.

Mandelbaum, Maurice (1948). A Critique of Philosophies of History. *The Journal of Philosophy* 45 (14): 365–78.

Marcelino, Douglas Attila (2021). Descobrir, Desapossar: ensaio sobre Michel de Certeau e o lugar da ética na teoria e na historiografia. *História da Historiografia* 14 (36): 45–72.

Marwick, Arthur (1989). *The Nature of History*, 3rd ed., Basingstoke: Macmillan.

Marwick, Arthur (2001). *The New Nature of History: Knowledge, Evidence, Language*, Basginstoke: Palgrave.

Mata, Sérgio da (2011). Historiografia, Normatividade, Orientação: Sobre o Substrato Moral do Conhecimento Histórico. In Fernando Nicolazzi, Helena Mollo, and Valdei Lopes de Araujo, eds., *Aprender com a História? O Passado e o Futuro de uma Questão*, Rio de Janeiro: Editora FGV, 2011, pp. 59–76.

Matute, Álvaro, ed. (2015). *La Teoría de la Historia en México (1940–1968)*, 2nd ed., *México*: Fondo de Cultura Económica.

Mbembe, Achille (2001). *On the Postcolony*, Berkeley: University of California Press.

McCullagh, C. Behan (1998). *The Truth of History*, London: Routledge.

McCullagh, C. Behan (2004). *The Logic of History: Putting Postmodernism in Perspective*, London: Routledge.

Megill, Allan (2007). *Historical Knowledge, Historical Error: A Contemporary Guide to Practice*, Chicago: The University of Chicago Press.

Mendiola, Alfonso (1993). Michel de Certeau: la búsqueda de la diferencia. *Historia y Grafía* 1: 9–31.

Menezes, Jonathan (2019). The Limits of the "Autumn of Historiography": On Frank Ankersmit's Postmodernist Moment. *Journal of the Philosophy of History* 15 (1): 84–105.

Menezes, Jonathan (2021). *Frank Ankersmit: A Metamorfose do Historicismo.* Londrina: Engenho das Letras.

Mignolo, Walter D. (2006). *The Idea of Latin America.* London: Blackwell Publishing.

Mignolo, Walter D. and Escobar, Arturo, eds. (2010). *Globalization and the Decolonial Option*, London: Routledge.

Mink, Louis O. (1979). Philosophy and Theory of History. In Georg G. Iggers and Harold T. Parker, eds., *International Handbook of Historical Studies: Contemporary Research and Theory*, Westport: Greenwood Press, pp. 17–27.

Mink, Louis O. (1987). *Historical Understanding*, Ithaca: Cornell University Press.

Miranda, Fernanda Rodrigues de and Assunção, Marcello Felisberto Morais de, eds. (2021). *Pensamento Afrodiaspórico em Perspectiva: Abordagens no Campo da História e da Literatura*, Porto Alegre: Editora Fi.

Mora Silva, Julimar del Carmen (2018). Utopias and Dystopias of Our History: Historiographical Approximation to "the Latin American" in the Mexican Social Thought of the twentieth Century (Edmundo O'Gorman, Guillermo Bonfil Batalla and Leopoldo Zea). *História Da Historiografia* 11 (28): 195–218.

Myers, Jorge, ed. (2008). *Historia de los Intelectuales en América Latina: La Ciudad Letrada, de la Conquista al Modernismo.* Vol I In *Historia de los Intelectuales en América Latina.* Buenos Aires: Katz Editores.

Nava Murcia, Ricardo (2019). Archivo y alteridad: "el otro" como lo espectral de la historiografia. *Historia y Grafía* 53: 79–107.

Nicolazzi, Fernando (2016). Raízes do Brasil e o ensaio histórico brasileiro: da história filosófica à síntese sociológica, 1836–1936. *Revista Brasileira de História* 36 (73): 89–110.

Nicolazzi, Fernando (2019). Os Historiadores e seus Públicos: Regimes Historiográficos, Recepção da História e História Pública. *Revista História Hoje* 8 (15): 203–22.

Noiriel, Gérard (1996). *Sur la "crise" de l'histoire*, Paris: Belin.

Nuccetelli, Susana (2020). *An Introduction to Latin American Philosophy*, Cambridge: Cambridge University Press.

Ohara, João Rodolfo Munhoz (2021a). Teoria da História: epistemologia, metodologia, teoria social …? In Marcelo de Mello Rangel and Augusto Bruno de Carvalho Dias Leite, eds., *História e Filosofia: Problemas Ético-políticos*, Vitória: Editora Milfontes, pp. 35–44.

Ohara, João Rodolfo Munhoz (2021b). Towards a Broad and Inclusive Theory and Philosophy of History. In *Geschichtstheorie am Werk*, Bielefeld, accessed on January 3, 2022, https://gtw.hypotheses.org/1241.

Oikión-Solano, Verónica (2011). Represión y tortura en México en la década de 1970. Un testimonio político. *Historia y Grafía* 37: 115–48.

Oliveira, Maria da Glória de (2018). Os Sons do Silêncio: Interpretações Feministas Decoloniais à História da Historiografia. *História da Historiografia* 11 (28): 104–40.

Oliveira, Rodrigo Perez (2018). O engajamento político e historiográfico no ofício dos historiadores brasileiros: uma reflexão sobre a fundação da historiografia brasileira contemporânea (1975–1979). *História da Historiografia* 11 (26): 197–222.

Ovalle Pastén, Daniel (2019). Actualidad en teoría de la historia. Una mirada desde las "relaciones con el pasado." *Autoctonía. Revista de Ciencias Sociales e Historia* 3 (1): 16–27.

Palti, Elías J. (2006). The Problem of "Misplaced Ideas" Revisited: Beyond the "History of Ideas" in Latin America. *Journal of the History of Ideas* 67 (1): 149–79.

Palti, Elías J. (2009). Beyond Revisionism: The Bicentennial of Independence, the Early Republican Experience, and Intellectual History in Latin America. *Journal of the History of Ideas* 70 (4): 593–614.

Palti, Elías J. (2018a). Beyond the "History of Ideas": The Issue of the "Ideological Origins of the Revolutions of Independence" Revisited. *Journal of the History of Ideas* 79 (1): 125–41.

Palti, Elías J. (2018b). El tópico de "los orígenes ideológicos" de las revoluciones de independencia como problema. Una relectura a partir de Tradición política española e ideología revolucionaria de Mayo, de Tulio Halperin Donghi. *História da Historiografia* 11 (27): 20–36.

Partner, Nancy (2013). Foundations: Theoretical Frameworks for Knowledge of the Past. In Nancy Partner and Sarah Foot, eds., *The SAGE Handbook of Historical Theory*, Los Angeles: SAGE, pp. 1–8.

Partner, Nancy and Foot, Sarah, eds. (2013). *The SAGE Handbook of Historical Theory*, Los Angeles: SAGE.

Paul, Herman (2011). *Hayden White: The Historical Imagination*, Cambridge: Polity Press.

Paul, Herman (2015a). *Key Issues in Historical Theory*, New York: Routledge.

Paul, Herman (2015b). Relations to the Past: A Research Agenda for Historical Theorists. *Rethinking History* 19 (3): 450–58.

Paul, Herman (2021). History and Philosophy of History (HPH): A Call for Cooperation. In Jouni-Matti Kuukkanen, ed., *Philosophy of History: Twenty-First-Century Perspectives*, London: Bloomsbury Academic, pp. 165–79.

Paul, Herman and Kleinberg, Ethan (2018). Are Historians Ontological Realists? An Exchange. *Rethinking History* 22 (4): 546–57.

Paul, Herman and van Veldhuizen, Adriaan (2018). A Retrieval of Historicism: Frank Ankersmit's Philosophy of History and Politics. *History and Theory* 57 (1): 33–55.

Pereira, Ana Carolina Barbosa (2018). Precisamos falar sobre o lugar epistêmico na Teoria da História. *Revista Tempo e Argumento* 10 (24): 88–114.

Pihlainen, Kalle (2017). *The Work of History: Constructivism and a Politics of the Past*, London: Routledge.

Potter, Elizabeth (2007). Feminist Epistemology and Philosophy of Science. In Linda Martín Alcoff and Eva Feder Kittay, eds., *The Blackwell Guide to Feminist Philosophy*, Malden: Blackwell, pp. 235–53.

Reed, Kate (2006). *New Directions in Social Theory: Race, Gender and the Canon*, London: SAGE.

Richardson, Alan (2015). From Troubled Marriage to Uneasy Collocation: Thomas Kuhn, Epistemological Revolutions, Romantic Narratives, and History and Philosophy of Science. In William J. Devlin and Alisa Bokulich, eds., *Kuhn's Structure of Scientific Revolutions – 50 Years On*, Cham: Springer, pp. 39–50.

Ricœur, Paul (1983). *Temps et Récit, Tome I*, Paris: Éditions du Seuil.

Ricœur, Paul (2000). *La Mémoire, l'Histoire, l'Oubli*, Paris: Éditions du Seuil.

Rigney, Ann (1990). *The Rhetoric of Historical Representation: Three Narrative Histories of the French Revolution*, Cambridge: Cambridge University Press.

Rorty, Richard (2000). Kuhn. In W. H. Newton-Smith, ed., *A Companion to the Philosophy of Science*, Malden: Blackwell, pp. 203–06.

Roth, Paul (1988). Narrative Explanations: The Case of History. *History and Theory* 27 (1): 1–13.

Roth, Paul (1992). Hayden White and the Aesthetics of Historiography. *History of the Human Sciences* 5 (1): 17–35.

Roth, Paul (2016). Back to the Future: Postnarrativist Historiography and Analytic Philosophy of History. *History and Theory* 55 (2): 270–81.

Roth, Paul (2018). Reviving Philosophy of History. In Krzysztof Brzechczyn, ed., *Towards a Revival of Analytical Philosophy of History: Around Paul A. Roth's Vision of Historical Sciences*, Leiden: Brill-Rodopi, pp. 9–27.

Roth, Paul (2020). *The Philosophical Structure of Historical Explanation*, Evanston: Northwestern University Press.

Rüsen, Jörn (1984). Theory of History in the Development of West German Historical Studies: A Reconstruction and Outlook. *German Studies Review* 7 (1): 11–25.

Rüsen, Jörn (2017). *Evidence and Meaning: A Theory of Historical Studies.* Translated by Diane Kerns and Katie Digan. New York: Berghahn.

Rüsen, Jörn (2020). A Turning Point in Theory of History: The Place of Hayden White in the History of Metahistory. *History and Theory* 59 (1): 92–102.

Salmon, Wesley C. (2000). Logical Empiricism. In W. H. Newton-Smith, ed., *A Companion to the Philosophy of Science*, Malden: Blackwell, pp. 233–42.

Sánchez León, Pablo and Izquierdo Martín, Jesús, eds. (2008). *El Fin de los Historiadores: Pensar Históricamente en el Siglo XXI*, Buenos Aires: Siglo XXI.

Sarlo, Beatriz (2005). *Tiempo Pasado: Cultura de la Memoria y Giro Subjetivo. Una Discusión*, Buenos Aires: Siglo XXI.

Schutte, Ofelia (1993). *Cultural Identity and Social Liberation in Latin American Thought*, Albany: State University of New York Press.

Schutte, Ofelia (2003). Continental Philosophy and Postcolonial Subjects. In Eduardo Mendieta, ed., *Latin American Philosophy: Currents, Issues, Debates*, Bloomington: Indiana University Press, pp. 150–62

Scott, Joan W. (1988). *Gender and the Politics of History*, New York: Columbia University Press.

Scott, Joan W. (2011). *The Fantasy of Feminist History*, Durham: Duke University Press.

Sebastiani, Silvia (2011). Las escrituras de la historia del Nuevo Mundo: Clavijero y Robertson en el contexto de la ilustración europea. *Historia y Grafía* 37: 203–36.

Seth, Sanjay (2004). Reason or Reasoning? Clio or Shiva? *Social Text* 22 (1): 85–101.

Simon, Zoltán Boldizsár (2019). Do Theorists of History Have a Theory of History? Reflections on a Non-Discipline. *História da Historiografia* 12 (29), 53–68.

Simon, Zoltán Boldizsár and Kuukkanen, Jouni-Matti (2015). Introduction: Assessing Narrativism. *History and Theory* 54 (2): 153–61.

Skodo, Admir (2013). Analytical Philosophy and the Philosophy of Intellectual History: A Critical Comparison and Interpretation. *Journal of the Philosophy of History* 7 (2): 137–61.

Smith, Bonnie G. (2000). *The Gender of History: Men, Women, and Historical Practice*, Cambridge, MA: Harvard University Press.

Smith, Nadia Clare (2006). *A "Manly Study"? Irish Women Historians, 1868-1949*, Basingstoke: Palgrave Macmillan.

Spivak, Gayatri Chakravorty (1999). *A Critique of Postcolonial Reason: Toward a History of the Vanishing Present*, Cambridge, MA: Harvard University Press.

Stern, Fritz, ed. (1970). *The Varieties of History: From Voltaire to the Present*, 2nd ed., London: Macmillan Education.

Swedberg, Richard (2016). Before Theory comes Theorizing or How to Make Social Science More Interesting. *The British Journal of Sociology* 67 (1): 5–22.

Táíwò, Olúfẹ́mi (1998). Exorcising Hegel's Ghost: Africa's Challenge to Philosophy. *African Studies Quarterly* 1 (4): 3–16.

Torstendahl, Rolf (2003). Fact, Truth, and Text: The Quest for a Firm Basis for Historical Knowledge Around 1900. *History and Theory* 42 (3): 305–31.

Tozzi, Verónica (2009). Hayden White y una filosofía de la historia literariamente informada. *Ideas y Valores* 140: 73–98.

Tozzi, Verónica (2012). The Epistemic and Moral Role of Testimony. *History and Theory* 51 (1): 1–17.

Tozzi, Verónica (2018). A Pragmatist View on Two Accounts of the Nature of Our "Connection" with the Past: Hayden White and David Carr Thirty Years Later. *Rethinking History* 22 (1): 65–85.

Tozzi, Verónica (2022). Narrativism. In Chiel van den Akker, ed., *The Routledge Companion to Historical Theory*, London: Routledge, pp. 113–28.

Trapp, Rafael Petry (2019). História, Raça e Sociedade: Notas sobre Descolonização e Historiografia Brasileira. *Revista de Teoria da História* 22 (2): 52–77.

Tucker, Aviezer (2001). The Future of the Philosophy of Historiography. *History and Theory* 40 (1): 37–56.

Tucker, Aviezer (2004). *Our Knowledge of the Past: A Philosophy of Historiography*. Cambridge: Cambridge University Press.

Tucker, Aviezer, ed. (2009). *A Companion to the Philosophy of Historiography*, Malden: Wiley-Blackwell.

Tucker, Aviezer (2010). Where Do We Go from Here? Jubilee Report on History and Theory. *History and Theory* 49 (4): 64–84.

Tyson, Sarah (2018). *Where Are the Women? Why Expanding the Archive Makes Philosophy Better*, New York: Columbia University Press.

Vallega, Alejandro A. (2014). *Latin American Philosophy from Identity to Radical Exteriority*, Bloomington: Indiana University Press.

van den Akker, Chiel, ed. (2022). *The Routledge Companion to Historical Theory*, London: Routledge.

Vann, Richard T. (1995). Turning Linguistic: History and Theory and History and Theory, 1960–1975. In Frank R. Ankersmit and Hans Hellner, eds., *A New Philosophy of History*, Chicago: The University of Chicago Press, pp. 40–69.

Vann, Richard T. (1998). The Reception of Hayden White. *History and Theory* 37 (2): 143–61.

Veyne, Paul (1978). *Comment on Écrit l'Histoire*, 2nd ed., Paris: Seuil.

Villalobos Álvarez, Rebeca (2017). Filosofía, Teoría o Metodología de la Historia: El Caso de Metahistoria de Hayden White (n. 1928). In Pilar Gilardi González and Martín F. Ríos Saloma, eds., *Historia y Método en el Siglo XX*. México: UNAM, pp. 175–96.

Von Leyden, Wolfgang (1958). Antiquity and Authority: A Paradox in the Renaissance Theory of History. *Journal of the History of Ideas* 19 (4): 473–92.

Walsh, Catherine E. and Mignolo, Walter (2018). *On Decoloniality*, Durham: Duke University Press.

Walsh, William H. (1960) [1951]. *Philosophy of History: An Introduction*, New York: Harper Torchbooks.

White, Deborah Gray, ed. (2008). *Telling Histories: Black Women Historians in the Ivory Tower*, Chapel Hill: The University of North Carolina Press.

White, Hayden (1973). *Metahistory: The Historical Imagination in Nineteenth-Century Europe*, Baltimore: The Johns Hopkins University Press.

White, Hayden (1986). *Tropics of Discourse: Essays in Cultural Criticism*, Baltimore: The Johns Hopkins University Press.

White, Hayden (1987). *The Content of the Form: Narrative Discourse and Historical Representation*, Baltimore: The Johns Hopkins University Press.

White, Hayden (1999). *Figural Realism: Studies in the Mimesis Effect*, Baltimore: The Johns Hopkins University Press.

White, Hayden (2014) *The Practical Past*, Evanston: Northwestern University Press.

White, Morton (1965). *Foundations of Historical Knowledge*, New York: Harper & Row.

Wiredu, Kwasi (1998). Toward Decolonizing African Philosophy and Religion. *African Studies Quarterly* 1 (4): 17–46.

Wiredu, Kwasi (2002). Conceptual Decolonization as an Imperative in Contemporary African Philosophy: Some Personal Reflections. *Rue Descartes* 36: 53–64.

Zammito, John (2009). Historians and the Philosophy of Historiography. In Aviezer Tucker, ed., *A Companion to the Philosophy of Historiography*, Malden: Wiley-Blackwell, pp. 63–84.

Zea, Leopoldo (1969). *La Filosofía Americana como Filosofía Sin Más*, México: Siglo XXI Editores.

Zea, Leopoldo (1978). *Filosofía de la Historia Americana*, México: Fondo de Cultura Económica.

Zermeño Padilla, Guillermo (2013). La Historiografía en México: Un Balance (1940–2010). *Historia Mexicana* 62 (4): 1695–742.

Zermeño Padilla, Guillermo (2020). Volver a Hayden White. *Historia y Grafía* 28 (55): 17–49.

Acknowledgments

I would like to thank the two referees for their generous reading and insightful observations. Writing in a new format like this is challenging, and their insights were essential in polishing the final version for publication. Of course, any remaining shortcomings are my own.

Cambridge Elements ≡

Historical Theory and Practice

Elements in the Series

The Theory and Philosophy of History: Global Variations
João Ohara

A full series listing is available at: www.cambridge.org/EHTP

Printed in the United States
by Baker & Taylor Publisher Services